Holy Bible

Holy Bible

Best God Damned Version

Genesis

Steve Ebling

Copyright © 2015 Steve Ebling

All rights reserved. No part of this publication may be reproduced or transmitted in any form or by any means, electronic or mechanical, including photocopying, recording, or any information storage and retrieval system, except for brief quotations in critical articles and reviews, without the prior written permission of the author.

Ebling, Steve.
Holy Bible : Best God Damned Version Genesis/ Steve Ebling
p. cm.
ISBN-10: 1508880522
ISBN-13: 978-1508880523
1. Ebling, Steve–Religion. 2. Religion–United States–Biblical Commentary. 3. Religion–United States–Agnosticism. 4. Religion–United States–Atheism. 5. Bibles–United States–Other Translations/General. 6. Humor–United States–Religion. I. Title.

Editing by: Julia Lee Bristow
Cover design by: Steve Ebling
Book design by: Julia Lee Bristow

Preface

The Bible is not the word of God

It is an ancient library of books (written over a span of 2,000 years by different authors, in different places, with different theologies and conceptions of God) that plagiarizes myths, legends, and stories that occur in a "world" that does not exist.

As for Genesis: Four original Hebrew source documents, written between 900 BC and 500 BC, were cut up around 450 BC and pasted into the irrational mess of duplicated stories, contradictions, lunacies, and impossibilities that became the first five books of the Bible (the Hebrew Torah and the Christian Pentateuch).

There is no consistent "God" character in these five books. He is the family god of Abraham or the tribal god of Moses or the national god of David, all destined to one day evolve into the one true God of the later prophets. His name is Yahweh or El or El Shaddai or some other variation of El, and he gets lost in the Garden of Eden or has lunch with Abraham or wrestles Jacob in the small picture, and he creates and rules the "world" in the big one, all depending on which fragment of what source is being repeated in any given story.

I followed the Jerusalem Bible because it uses the ancient god names. In Genesis his name might change between paragraphs and sentences and sometimes even within a sentence, so expect some confusion.

Every version of the Bible ever written weasel-words around and glosses over its inherent stupidity. I am writing a complete version of the Bible that does precisely the opposite. My "Best God Damned Version" of the

Bible will celebrate biblical stupidity for atheists, agnostics, and anyone else who enjoys its exposition and ridicule.

So thanks for taking a look. I hope you enjoy the read and that you learn something from it. I have established an email address for your own thoughts and comments and I hope you will use it. If you are thoughtful and sane, I will respond to you.

Steve Ebling
bgdBible@gmail.com

Genesis

Chapter 1

A Creation Story

"In the beginning God created the heaven and the earth."

So the Bible begins and right away I have a gripe. The Hebrew word translated here as "God" is "elohim" and elohim is plural, so the first verse of the Bible should actually read:

"In the beginning gods created the heaven and the earth."

This is no small thing. The difference between God, capital G, and gods, small g, is the difference between monotheism and polytheism. It's fun to watch the apologists dance around this inconvenient fact. Their best explanation is that "God is so great that he cannot be expressed as a singularity."

Do you like that one? It's like saying that Abraham Lincoln was so great that Abraham Lincolns gave the Gettysburg Address!

Preposterous.

But let's get back to the famous seven days of Creation:

Day 1. The world was a formless spill of water. God "let" light shine on it to create day and night and I have no idea where this light came from (there being no sun, moon or stars yet) or how the day/night part worked without any sunset or sunrise, but that's what the Bible says.

Day 2. God created a vault, a solid dome in the water to make space for the world (kind of like inflating a balloon underwater, with our "world" inside the balloon, surrounded by the water) and he named the vault "heaven."

What?

I thought heaven was this fabulous theme park where you lived forever in perfect happiness with God and he picked up every check?

Sorry.

Heaven, originally at least, is just the blue expanse of sky sitting over the flat, circular earth like a cup turned over a saucer, and yes it's solid, it has to be, because it's holding back the primal water above while the earth somehow floats or sits on the water below.

Day 3. God collected the water below heaven into the seas and allowed dry land to appear. It seems you would have to reduce the amount of water on earth to allow dry land to appear, but the Bible doesn't say, and maybe God "let dry land appear" the same way he let light appear, something he could do just because he's God and is not required to make sense. Anyhow, as soon as the land appeared, plants and trees and bushes and grasses sprouted upon it, and don't ask me how this occurred without sunlight. I guess God made due with the original mystery light from day one and, by the way, what ever happened to that original mystery light? Did the batteries run out or what?

Whatever; there were now two elements in the world: Heaven and Earth.

Day 4. God created the sun, moon, and stars and installed them in the dome of heaven. The two big lights, the sun and the moon, governed day and night. All that was left now was for God to create life on the earth and he got right to it.

Day 5. God created all the plants and animals that live in the seas and he probably tinkered with the water temperature to get it just right.

Day 6. God created all the land animals and the "birds of heaven" and then, for the grand finale, he announced:

"Let us make man look just like us and let them be masters of life on earth!"

Huh?
Let *us* make man?

Just another reference to gods having created the world, so don't worry, just understand that God's or the gods' creation was done and it was time for ... drum roll, please ... God's famous day of rest!

Day 7. God's lounging in a hammock, eyes closed, gin and tonic resting on his belly, bathing in the heavenly light, a big contented smile on his face after a hard week's work.

Bible says here:

"Thus heaven and earth were completed with all their array."

But wait...

Get that lazy prick God up out of his hammock! Turns out, there is a second Creation Story! It begins right after the first one ends, and sure, they contradict each other, especially in the sequence of events involved in the creation.

Chapter 2

Another Creation Story

The second creation story begins at Genesis 2:4.

The first thing you notice is that God's name has changed from Elohim to YHWH, the Hebrew theonym commonly referred to as the Tetragrammaton, which is Greek for (what else) "four letters."

So how do you pronounce YHWH?

You don't.

Originally, God's name was considered too sacred to speak, so in ancient Hebrew it is the properly unpronounceable: YHWH. Although, just to offend God, I tried to pronounce it, but the sound I made didn't amount to much of an insult. Even when I yelled it, all it did was give me a sore throat. This probably explains why so many depictions of the ancient Israelites show them clutching theirs. A couple thousand years later they decided it was okay to pronounce God's name so they bought a couple of vowels, inserted them into YHWH and made it "Yahweh." I'll call YHWH "Yahweh" in this Bible so you can read it aloud to your kids without hurting your throats. Just remember, whenever you read "Yahweh," technically it's "YHWH."

The second version of the Creation Story begins with a barren, waterless, rainless, and vacant earth. YHWH—I mean Yahweh—got right to work:

He made water flow up from the ground to irrigate the earth. He made Man out of dirt and breathed life into his nostrils. He planted the Garden of Eden in the east and put Man in it. He made trees grow in the Garden, including the "Tree of Life" and the "Tree of the Knowledge of Good and Evil" and he ran rivers through the Garden.

Then Yahweh commanded Man, "You can eat from any tree in the Garden except the 'Tree of the Knowledge of Good and Evil.' If you eat from that tree, I will kill you!"

That's right, Yahweh, who will forever judge us on our performance of good or evil, did not want us to know the difference between them! And was so dead serious about it that he told Man he would kill him if he ate the fruit and learned it!

Seems a little counter-productive, doesn't it?

Anyhow, Yahweh pitied poor Man being alone and decided to make a "helper" for him and preferably one he could fuck. He made animals out of dirt and he let Man name them—I don't know if he marched the animals by Man or had a slide show or what, the Bible doesn't say—and Man named them, but he was not willing to fuck any one of them, so Yahweh put Man to sleep, ripped one of his ribs out and made Woman from it. It was like waking up in Mexico without a kidney and you would think Man would be in terrible pain when he woke, but he felt just fine, and Yahweh introduced him to Woman.

Man took one look at that first set of tits and blurted, "You're goddamn right that's Woman!"

All right, it didn't exactly go that way, but Man did spew some nonsense about this helper being made from him, so he named it/her "Woman," even though God had already introduced it/her as "Woman," and how Man and Woman were designed to become one flesh again, blah, blah, blah, but I guarantee you that whatever he was babbling, he was fixated on her tits and couldn't wait to fuck her!

And you women can learn something here: You're not here to cause trouble, do you hear me? You're here to help the men! The Bible is very clear about this: You are "helpers!" Please remember it the next time you want to mouth off!

His creation finished, God gave Man and Woman simple instructions: "I built Paradise for you. Take good care of it and live happily in it, without any knowledge of anything."

Without any ... huh?

That's right, God wanted us to live in paradise without knowing one goddamned thing about anything! We got paradise in exchange for ignorance and I'm not talking about the piss-poor, watered-down ignorance we see on earth today, I'm talking about pure goddamned ignorance! As in, we don't know if we just pissed on our feet or not. That, and we can't eat the best fruit in the Garden, you know, the one that provides precisely the knowledge God forbids us to have?

I won't even mention how sadistic that is.

Anyhow, this completes the second creation story. I considered both versions and thought: God made the "world" and all the plants and animals, including us, that live in it. Well, okay, so far, so good, but get this: When God created animals, including us, he made it so we have to kill and eat each other to survive!

How sick is that?

But wait, that's not all! Not only do we have to kill and eat each other, we have to digest each other into shit and squeeze warm, stinking piles of it out of our asses!

I'd like to see God selling that life plan to the Chamber of Commerce!

And what does that tell you about God's character? He's God, for Chrissake! Could have made us any goddamn way he wanted. Could have made us run on sunlight or air or batteries or, let's face it, nothing at all. But, no! This prick makes us have to eat each other and convert each other into stinking piles of shit just to stay alive!

You think about that.

And well, I have one more little complaint, barely worth mentioning, but I will. If God made Man and all of the other animals from dirt, he could have made Woman from dirt too, and saved Man a rib, that's all I'm saying.

You, on the other hand, might say, "Ah, excuse me, I just read not one, but two versions of the Creation and I listened to your rant about eating and turning each other into shit, but what I want to know is:

Where the fuck is the universe?

Well, you asked the right question, but I'm sorry to tell you that there is no universe in the Bible. Go stand on the eastern shore of the Mediterranean Sea. Draw a circle around you a couple thousand miles in diameter. That big flat circle is the biblical "earth." Now, place the solid blue dome of heaven (the sky) over this "earth" and you have the biblical "world."

The Bible thinks we live in a goddamn terrarium! The earth is the floor and the heaven is the dome. The primal water exists above the heaven and below the earth. God opens windows in the heaven when he wants it to rain on us and springs gurgle up from below the earth. The sun, moon, and stars are skylights. There are no continents, no other places or climates, no Atlantic or Pacific oceans in a Bible that does not accurately describe anything more than one lousy donkey ride from the Mediterranean Sea.

Consider this: God spent five days creating the earth and one day creating the rest of the universe. Does that make sense? The universe exists for fifteen billion light years in every direction we can see. There are trillions upon trillions upon trillions of stars in it, for Chrissake! A grain of sand is a far bigger percentage of the earth than the earth is of the universe. By a factor of about a gazillion! And we have no idea where the universe ends, or if it ends, and we can only guess as to what might exist beyond it.

That's a whole lot of ignorance!

I'm sorry to spend so much time on this, but it's a sore spot for me. I'm tired of morons telling me that Genesis is a valid creation story. Genesis is a fucking cartoon—plagiarized from a Babylonian cartoon that they plagiarized from a Sumerian cartoon—our best guess as to who we are and where we came from at a time when we knew absolutely nothing about anything!

All right, I'm done ranting.

The second chapter of Genesis ends with Man and Woman living blissfully ignorant and shamelessly naked in the Garden of Eden.

Chapter 3

A talking snake spoils Yahweh's plan for perpetual human ignorance

A snake, the most subtle (and where else is a snake ever described as being subtle?) of all the wild animals that Yahweh made, appeared and asked Woman, "Did God really say you can't eat from any tree in the garden?"

"Oh no! We can eat from any tree but the Tree of the Knowledge of Good and Evil," Woman explained, "but if we eat from that tree or even touch it, God will kill us!"

"That bastard!" thought the snake and he spat, "Bullshit! This fruit will not kill you! God knows that if you eat from that tree you will open your eyes and become like gods and know the difference between good and evil!"

Become like gods! Well, isn't that interesting...

"Fuck God! Eat all you want, learn all you can, write a goddamn encyclopedia for Chrissake!"

"Well," Woman thought, "It's a beautiful tree and the fruit looks delicious and who better to trust than a talking snake?" Abandoning all caution, she picked some forbidden fruit and shared it with Man.

They each took a bite...

Flash!

Man suddenly felt the cool breeze on his balls and looked frantically at Woman...

She looked frantically at him...

Holy shit! We're buck fucking naked!

The realization staggered them and somehow it came packaged with the idea that being naked was sinful. Now they scrambled desperately to find something, anything they could wear for clothing, even though they had no idea what clothing was. They settled on fig leaves that they quickly sewed into loin cloths and don't ask me what they used for a needle and thread or how they knew how to sew—the Bible doesn't say.

Yahweh walks into the Garden of Eden

Just then, Yahweh walked into the garden, prowling, looking for Man and Woman, and as soon as they heard him, they ran and hid among some trees.

Yahweh looked everywhere, but could not find his two prized creations. Finally, exasperated, he yelled, "Man! Where in hell are you?"

The suddenly-become-like-gods couple emerged sheepishly from the trees, naked but for their fig leaves.

Man mumbled, "I heard you in the garden and I was, well, I was afraid because I'm naked, so I hid."

Well, Yahweh's no dummy; he understood immediately. "And how did you know you were naked? Hmmm? Has someone been eating forbidden fruit?"

Here is some insight into the different God characters in the Bible. He is, at various times, a family god, a tribal god, a national god, the chief god, and eventually the one-and-only God, depending on what document sourced the story and who wrote it, when and where. This version of Yahweh is from an early source. A later version of God would have known these two fools ate the forbidden fruit because he knows goddamn everything, but this Yahweh does not and has to ask.

Man blurted, "Well...all right! I ate the forbidden fruit!" And then he threw Woman under the bus, "But she made me do it!"

Yahweh glared at Woman. "Why did you disobey me?" he demanded.

Now Woman threw the snake under the bus. "That damn snake talked me into it."

So now Yahweh turned and cursed the snake, "For this, you will crawl on your belly and eat dust like...well, like a fucking snake! Forever! You and Woman will hate each other and her children will stomp your children's heads and your children will strike their heels!"

You wonder, did the snake originally have legs and maybe once won "Dancing with the Snakes?" And did Yahweh just grab him and rip off his legs? Forcing him to slither away on his belly like, well, like a fucking snake?

Or what? The Bible doesn't say. Nor does it say where the tame animals came from, there being only two potential animal tamers alive and I haven't read about any animal taming yet.

Whatever the story was, now Yahweh addressed Woman, "And you! Because you ate the forbidden fruit, I sentence you and all women to suffer horrible pain during childbirth. You'll think you're birthing goddamn Buicks! And I mean forever! And a woman's only job will be to love and obey her husband!"

Now, finally, Yahweh turned to Man, "Because you listened to Woman and ate the forbidden fruit, I curse your soil! Do you hear me? Every crop you plant will grow into inedible crap until the day you die and return to the dirt you're made of!" Yahweh spat. "For dirt you were and to dirt you shall return!"

And that was it.

Man took this happy occasion to name Woman "Eve" because she would become everyone's mother and after Yahweh finished his tirade, he calmed right down and tailored wonderful skin tunics for Man and Woman and dressed them up right good and proper.

Yahweh kicks Man and Eve out of Paradise

Then Yahweh (apparently back up in heaven or above heaven or wherever in hell he lives) said to his friends (whoever and whatever in hell they are), "The fools ate from the Tree of Knowledge and learned good from evil! Next they'll eat from the Tree of Life and live forever, just like us! We can't have that, so I'm bouncing them from Paradise!"

So Yahweh banished Man and Woman from the Garden of Eden and posted great winged creatures to prevent their return and he installed a fiery flashing sword to guard the Tree of Life. The story ends here and it tells a lot about God's character: He made the animals have to kill and eat each other to survive and he will reward us for doing good and punish us for doing evil, but did not want us to know the difference between them.
 What kind of a fuck-job deal is that?
 Did he want us to bounce around the Garden of Eden like naked human bumper cars? Performing random acts of good and evil, unable to distinguish between them? Laughing at our hopeless attempts to live without knowledge? Were we to be some three-dimensional reality show that he and his buddies could watch in his basement?
 Or what?
 And what if we never ate the forbidden fruit? Fast forward a few thousand years. Would we still be stumbling around naked in the Garden of Eden? Knowing absolutely nothing about anything? And right there in the middle of the garden is this beautiful tree, the absolute centerpiece of the garden, with the most delicious fruit there is that provides precisely the knowledge he forbid us to have!

And we can't eat it?
What kind of a sadistic prick is this God?

Chapter 4

Cain and Abel

Man had two sons, Cain and Abel. Cain became a farmer and Abel became a shepherd and they were both good guys who tried to treat Yahweh right; Cain gave Yahweh a cut of his first harvest and Abel gave Yahweh the firstborn of his flock, with a side order of fat.

Yahweh pisses on Cain so he kills Abel

You might think Yahweh was very happy with both boys, but no. Yahweh loved Abel's gift of meat, probably because there's nothing better than a side order of fat, but he didn't give a rat's ass about Cain's gift of produce and he pissed on it.

When this broke Cain's heart, Yahweh explained, "When you do not do right, sin is hiding behind your door," which makes no goddamn sense, but his message was clear: When two people both do something equally nice for you, reward one and piss on the other, with a senseless explanation as to why you are doing it.

Poor Cain was so depressed that he took Abel out into the country and killed him.

What?

That's right, Cain brutally killed his brother Abel! And when he returned home and Yahweh asked him where his brother was, Cain just shrugged and wisecracked, "How do I know? Am I my brother's keeper?"

But Yahweh, sharp as ever, realized now that Cain had killed his brother (never mind that he's God and should know everything instantly).

He said to Cain, "So you killed your brother, did you? Well now I curse you: Your crops will be crap and you will wander the earth restlessly until you die!"

It was the same curse he gave Adam, plus the restless wandering part, and there were only three people alive then, so unless Eve had a nice little garden, I guess they ate a lot of meat in those early years.

Now Cain complained to Yahweh, "I can't stand this! You made me an outcast so now I must hide. Anyone who sees me will kill me!"

Again, there are only two other people alive and they're his parents; who is going to kill him?

"All right," Yahweh relented. "I'll fuck over anyone who kills you seven times! How's that?"

And he put a mark on Cain, perhaps a "Do Not Kill" tattoo, so his parents would not kill him.

Inexplicably, Cain did not end up wandering the earth restlessly; he settled in Nod, east of Eden, married and had kids, who had kids, who had kids, who had kids, and so on, for enough generations to populate the earth. And don't ask me where in hell Cain's wife came from; I do not believe you could mail-order a bride from Russia in those days, and the Bible doesn't say.

Chapter 5

A List of Adam's Descendants

This chapter stars God, not Yahweh. It obviously has a different author or authors than Chapter 4 and it's a little confusing, so I'll quote the beginning verbatim:

"God created Man in the likeness of God, both male and female, he blessed them and gave them the name Man" (5:1-2).

I guess technically, at least here, "Man" refers to all human beings, but who really cares? I won't bother listing all Adam's descendants, but trust me, neither Cain nor Abel is on the list because this version of Adam's progeny comes from a different source. Here, Adam is 130 years old when Woman gives birth to his first son, Seth, and Adam then fathers sons and daughters for the next 800 years to get the world population rolling.

It seems odd that God waited until Adam was 130 before he started giving him children, but this established the original biblical standard. Seth had his first son at 105 and none of Adam's progeny father anybody before they are at least 90 and all of them live to be 800 to 900 years old. Methuselah lived the longest of all: 969 years, and one of his sons, Lamech, was 187 years old when he fathered Noah and when Noah was 500 years old, he fathered Shem, Ham and Japheth.

Enough of this nonsense.
On to the famous story of Noah's Ark.

Chapter 6

The Sons of God Fuck our Women and they Birth Giants

Eventually, there were so many humans that Yahweh decided to limit our lifespan to 120 years to control the population. Meanwhile, the "sons of God," whoever and whatever in hell they are or were, saw our beautiful women and came down from heaven or wherever in hell they live or lived and fucked them, fathering the Nephilim, the giants and heroes of old, whoever and whatever in hell they were.

I have no idea how many "sons of God" we're talking, ten? A thousand? A million? Who knows? And did they just appear on earth? Or float down from the sky? And did our women throw themselves at them and spread their legs? Or did they knock on doors and say, "Hello, we're god's sons, we've come down from heaven or wherever in hell we live to fuck your women!"

Don't know.

The Bible sees this story of incredible beings appearing and fucking our women and fathering giants as being fairly incidental and not worthy of much explanation.

So be it.

God decides to drown us

We do know that whoever the "sons of god" were and however many of our women they fucked and however many giants were born in consequence, Yahweh looked around and saw nothing but wickedness and realized his prized Creation had gone horribly wrong.

And he thought, "Fuck it, I'll just kill the bastards and be done with them!"

Never mind that Yahweh, being God, could have changed the wicked to good with the snap of a holy finger. Apparently, he was so disgusted with humanity that he decided to just convert the earth into a giant toilet and flush us down it like so many unloved goldfish.

Except for one thing...

There was this one good guy, Noah.

God tracked him down and explained, "The life on earth is worthless, so I'm going to drown every human being except you and your family, so build an ark, take your family and a male and female of every animal there is onto it, load it up with provisions for all, and I'll look after you."

God gave Noah the exact specifications for the ark and Noah built it.

Chapter 7

Noah's Ark

Yahweh said to Noah, "You're the only good guy left on earth. Load your family on the ark and take seven pairs of every clean animal and bird and one pair of every unclean animal there is and take them onto the ark with you. In seven days, I will flood the earth and kill everything."

You'll notice this kind of repeats the end of chapter six, but with different numbers and the addition of "unclean" animals. In chapter six, it was just one pair of every animal and now it is seven pairs of clean animals and one pair of unclean animals. That's because two versions of the Flood Story collide here. The older version stars Yahweh and the newer one stars God (Elohim). The concept of "unclean" animals did not exist in the time of the older source, but did in the time of the newer one, so it's a little confusing.

Anyhow...

Noah was 600 years old when he boarded the ark with his family and all the animals. Then the springs of the great deep below the earth burst up through the ground, the windows of the heaven above opened, and water surged up from below and poured down from above and the great flood came, lifting the ark off the ground and floating it away. The flood waters rose until they covered the mountains and every living thing on earth drowned, except for Noah and his passengers.

I, of course, wonder about the fish. How do you drown a fish? It seems to me that all the fish must have survived God's preposterous flood just fine or maybe they all died when the salt water got mixed up with the fresh water?

Well, it's not worth considering.

Chapter 8

The Flood

I gave up trying to figure out how long Noah's cruise lasted, study chapters six to eight and do the math if you want, but it's impossible to compute a singular conclusion and who cares? The entire earth was never flooded anyhow for two simple reasons: The primal, infinite waters above the heaven (sky) and below the earth do not exist and there is not enough water on earth to flood it to a depth of an inch, much less to twenty-nine thousand feet.

Period.

End of argument.

This story simply plagiarizes a Sumerian myth about a horrible flood that covered enough land to make it seem to the locals like the whole world was flooded. It stars a guy named Utnapishtim as Noah and is essentially the same story and so obviously a myth and nothing actual that I won't waste any more time on it. If you're interested, Google: "Utnapishtim Noah Flood" and have at it.

Anyhow...

However long the flood lasted, God finally turned off the water and it began to subside. Noah released a raven and it flew around, but found nowhere to land and returned. Then Noah released a dove and it found no land and returned. Then, on the first day of the tenth month, the mountaintops appeared.

A week later, Noah released the dove again and this time it returned with an olive leaf in its beak. After another week, he released the dove and this time it did not return and then the ark came to rest among the mountains of Ararat.

On the first day of the first month, the waters began drying out on earth and Noah opened a hatch in the ark, looked out, and saw dry land on the twenty-seventh day of the second month.

God said to Noah, "You and your family can leave the ark now and let the animals out so they can swarm the earth and multiply."

Noah built an altar and incinerated clean animals and birds as burnt offerings to Yahweh, who loved smelling the sacrifices and thought, "I will never curse humans for being born evil or kill all of them again. As long as the earth endures, it will have planting and harvests and cold and heat and seasons."

I, of course, ask, "If God created us evil, why in hell was he surprised when we turned out to be evil?"

And about the two flood stories:

They agree that Yahweh/God (Elohim) got fed up with humanity and drowned everybody except Noah and his crew, but they disagree on most of the particulars.

I have some thoughts about this epic nonsense.

Couldn't God—being God—have just killed every human being he wanted to kill with just a thought? Or simply made us just disappear and eliminate the ghastly mess of millions of bloated corpses, rotting and stinking all over the earth after the flood?

And where did all the flood water go? I mean, the whole earth was under water, mountains and all. The Bible says all this extra water came from rain and from under the ground and, sure, that's impossible, but let's pretend that it's not and that it all came from the original creation water that gushed up from below the earth and poured down from above the heaven.

Okay.

Where in hell did the water go after the flood was over? All that water couldn't simply evaporate in a few days and it's not like the earth has a drain.

And wouldn't the salt water and fresh water get all mixed up in the flood? How did they separate after it subsided? I don't see that being explained.

Well, whatever; I'm just saying that God could have figured out a better way to kill us, is all. That he chose to cruelly drown all the people and animals makes you wonder about the prick. When you have God doing something that any human being with an IQ north of 60 can do better and smarter, you got a lousy god!

Chapter 9

God's Deal with Noah

After the Flood, God became Mr. Wonderful and blessed Noah and his sons.

"Get busy and populate the earth, boys!" he chirped. "The world is your oyster! Eat anything that moves and all the plants, eat anything but meat with blood in it, and don't kill other men because men look just like me." Never mind that God had just killed everyone else on earth; now he promised Noah, "I will never flood the earth again!"

And God invented rainbows and put one up in the sky. "Rainbows signify my promise to you. Whenever I see one, I'll be reminded to never drown everyone on earth again."

Happy days were here again.

You would think that after the flood subsided there would be millions of bloated, rotting, stinking corpses strewn everywhere, but in the Bible everything appears to be fine. You get the feeling that the sun was shining and birds were chirping and there was the newly-installed, feel-good rainbow glowing across the sky. Noah and his sons, Shem, Ham, and Japheth (he never had one named Curly as so many think) and their wives and families were now the only people on earth, and you wonder how many people they were—I mean, Noah was over six hundred years old, for Chrissake, and must have had at least 30 generations of grandkids, probably thousands of people, but the Bible doesn't say.

However many there were, the Bible says they were all on the ark, so the story becomes progressively stupider and more impossible the more you consider it, but we'll accept the Bible saying that Noah had just three sons and I guess they had wives and they all oiled up their crotches and got busy repopulating the earth.

Noah–our first confirmed alcoholic

Noah became a farmer and he was the first guy to grow grapes and make wine that he apparently liked to drink, because one day his son Ham stopped by Noah's tent and found him passed out drunk and naked, I guess on the floor.

Ham was horrified and ran right out and reported to his brothers.

Back at dad's tent, Shem and Japheth were more circumspect. There apparently was some unexplained, unofficial prohibition against seeing your father passed out drunk and naked, so Shem and Japheth stumbled backwards into Noah's tent and covered his naked body with a cloak. How they did this without seeing Noah or tripping over him is beyond me, but, as always, I will not be picky. The point is that Ham saw Noah passed out drunk and naked and Shem and Japheth did not.

Noah curses his grandchildren because Ham saw him passed out drunk and naked

When Noah woke from his drunken stupor and learned what Ham had "done to him" (saw him passed out drunk and naked), he became enraged.

"I curse Canaan!" he cried. "He will be his brothers' miserable slave!"

Huh?

Noah got drunk and passed out naked. All Ham did was find him. This was Ham's great crime? And for it,

Noah cursed Ham's son, Canaan, who will father the "Promised Land" that God will one day give to the Israelites?

We have multilevel stupidity at play here.

First, Ham saw his father passed out drunk and naked. What kind of crime is that? How do you look at someone and not see him? If you were to fine Ham five shekels for this "crime" it would be outrageous!

But all right, we'll play along. It's a crime to see your father passed out drunk and naked and Ham's guilty.

Why does Noah punish Ham's son and not Ham?

Ham committed the heinous crime of finding his father passed out drunk and naked. Why let him off and sentence his grandchildren, the Canaanites, to be slaughtered by his other grandchildren, the Israelites, instead?

This is stupid beyond belief!

One more thing.

This story establishes a biblical precedent: spare the actual criminal and punish his children instead. You encounter this lunacy repeatedly in the Torah/Old Testament and not once is it ever just or rational.

Anyhow, Noah lived another 350 years after the flood and died when he was 950 years old.

Chapter 10

Noah's Descendants

This chapter lists the descendants of Noah's sons Shem, Ham and Japheth, and the countries and nations they founded after the flood, including Canaan, which stretched from Sidon to Gerar near Gaza and to Sodom, Gomorrah, Adamah and Zeboiim near Lesha.

Nothing interesting here, so let's just move on.

Chapter 11

Yahweh makes everyone speak a different language because some guys built a tower

Some of Noah's descendants moved east, settled in the land of Shinar and built a city with a tower that reached up to the heaven. When they finished, Yahweh showed up to personally inspect their work and was so horrified by what he saw that when he returned home, wherever in hell home was or is, he reported:

They're one people, with one language and they can do goddamn anything! Nothing is impossible for these bastards! (11:6)

Consider Yahweh's concern.
He originally wanted us so ignorant that we could not tell right from wrong, but Man and Eve ate the fruit and acquired knowledge and now we had so much of it that we actually built a city with a tower—imagine that! And Yahweh's so blown away by this magnificent accomplishment that he figured now we could do just about goddamn anything and this scared him. But he had a plan that he shared with his buddies:

We'll go down and confuse the bastards until they can't understand each other. (11:7-8)

And they came down and gave every person on earth a different language and the town was named Babel in consequence, although, when you think about it, it would only have been called "Babel" in one language. Now everybody had a different language, so I'm not sure how that nonsense worked.

Another thing you wonder is why did Yahweh and his buddies have to come down here to confuse our language? Couldn't they have done this directly from heaven or wherever in hell they lived? I can't remember God coming down to earth to do anything, can you?

But this is mere observation.

My real complaint is what Yahweh did here and why. Some of us build a city with a tower and Yahweh punishes all of us by instantly making everyone speak a different language?

Are you fucking kidding me?

Imagine it is 4:00 in the afternoon and everything is fine. The clock ticks 4:01. Suddenly you can't understand the person talking to you and he or she can't understand you! You freak out and run outside. No one can understand anyone and everyone is freaked out and it's the same all over the world.

Think of the chaos!

Then, just to make things worse, Yahweh scatters everybody, each with his or her own new language, all over the earth.

Imagine that nightmare.

You're making your way to you don't know where and you don't know why you're going there and you can't understand anyone you meet along the way!

And for what?

Because some of us built a city with a tower? Again, are you fucking kidding me? For this, Yahweh made it so no one could understand anyone else?

Not exactly the act of a kind and loving god.

The chapter concludes with another, more lengthy genealogy of Shem's descendants and ends with Terah ordering his son Abram and his family to move to

Canaan, but for some reason they stopped en route and settled in Haran.

Chapter 12

Yahweh gives Abram Canaan, but Abram goes to Egypt instead and lets Pharaoh fuck his wife

Abram was 75 years old and he lived in Haran with his wife Sarai and his nephew Lot.

Yahweh told Abram, "Move to Canaan and I'll make you a great nation! I'll bless you and you'll be famous and I'll curse any bastard that curses you and everyone will kiss your ass!"

Well, hell yeah!

Abram rounded up his people and they all moved to Canaan and settled in Shechem and Yahweh appeared to Abram at the Oak of Moreh and said, "I'm giving you this land for your descendants."

Now the gift of an entire country is pretty generous, I mean, I don't think even Elvis ever gave anyone a country, did he? It was also a little presumptuous of Yahweh, because Canaan belonged to the god El, so it was kind of like the King of France saying, "Happy Birthday, I'm giving you England!"

But, no matter.

Abram built an altar for Yahweh at the Oak and another between Bethel and Ai and invoked Yahweh's name at both. But his enthusiasm for his new very own country quickly waned when he looked around and saw nothing but people turning black and puking themselves to death from plague.

Nope.

Abram rounded up his clan and they ran straight for Egypt! En route, Abram told his wife, "Look, you're a piece of ass, and I don't want any Egyptian killing me so he can fuck you, so you just tell them you're my sister, OK?"

Abram figured if the Egyptians thought Sarai was his sister they would just fuck her and leave him alone and I understand Sarai was ninety years old and that none of this makes any sense on any level, but that's what the Bible says.

So Abram, his "sister," Lot and the gang rode into Egypt and, sure enough, when Pharaoh learned there was a new piece of ass in town and barely 90 years old, he grabbed Sarai for his harem and for Abram it was as if he'd won an Egyptian game show. He got flocks, donkeys, oxen, camels, slaves and everything you could want for a great life in Egypt, all out of Pharaoh's gratitude for the use of his ninety-year-old "sister."

Meanwhile, I'm thinking Pharaoh was banging Sarai in his palace, behind the pyramids, under the Sphinx, rolling through piles of camel shit and anything else and it was all fine with Abram, who was happy as a clam with his prize winnings.

But guess who wasn't happy?

That's right, Yahweh!

He was so pissed about Pharaoh banging old Sarai like a 2-shekel whore that he infected Pharaoh's entire household with plague.

Please stop and consider that horror: high fever, seizures, vomiting blood, unquenchable thirst, until your body turns black and rots and you die hideously in intolerable pain! Yet God dispenses this nightmare throughout the Torah with the carelessness of a second grade teacher making a cutup stand in the corner.

I don't know how Pharaoh figured out that Sarai was Abram's wife and that Yahweh was punishing him for banging her all over Egypt, the Bible doesn't say and, frankly, I doubt Pharaoh even knew who Yahweh was or gave one rat's ass about him, but he somehow figured it out and got pissed and summoned Abram.

Pharaoh yells at Abram

Abram appeared immediately.
"Why tell me your wife is your sister and let me fuck her all over Egypt?" Pharaoh demanded. "Here!" He shoved Sarai back to Abram. "Take your wife back and get the fuck out of my country!"

For some reason, Pharaoh did not kill Abram. Keeping with the Bible theme of nothing you read makes much sense, Pharaoh gave Abram his limping, dripping wife back, kicked them out of Egypt, and they got to keep all their prize winnings.

Chapter 13

Abram returns to Canaan and Yahweh gives it to him again

Abram left Egypt as a rich man, returned to a now plague-free Canaan and checked in with Yahweh at the altar between Bethel and Ai. Lot was with him and a dispute broke out between Lot's and Abram's herdsmen and it became clear that the place was not big enough for both of them to coexist.

Abram told Lot, "We're family and we don't need trouble, so look around you and pick a direction. Whichever you choose, I'll choose the opposite and we'll go our separate ways."

Lot surveyed the landscape and saw that the Jordan plain was a beautifully-irrigated, ready-to-inhabit paradise.

"Ah, I'll take the Jordan plain," he said with a straight face.

And he took his people and settled there near the city of Sodom.

After Lot left, Yahweh said to Abram, "Look around you, I give you everything you can see, for as far as you can see, for you and your descendants, forever."

Abram did not say either: "I thought you just gave half of it to Lot?" or "I know, you already gave me Canaan, but thanks for giving it to me again."

He merely settled by the Oak of Mamre at Hebron and built an altar to Yahweh there, even though he had already settled and built one there when he first arrived in Canaan.

Chapter 14

Abram Rescues Lot

Meanwhile war broke out among some local kings. The kings of Sodom and Gomorrah fell into tar pits and their enemies captured everything they owned, though I've never heard of any other king losing anything because he fell into a tar pit, but so be it.

These kings also captured Lot and all of his people.

When Abram learned it, he rounded up 318 men and they went and routed Lot's enemies in a night raid, chasing them all the way to Hobah, north of Damascus, and Abraham recaptured all of Lot's women and children and wealth and gave Lot his life back.

When Abram returned home with the spoils of war, the king of Sodom crawled up out of the tar pit and met him in the Valley of Shaveh (Valley of the King) with Melchizedek, king of Salem and priest of "God Most High," who brought bread and wine and blessed Abram.

Abram offered Melchizedek a tenth of the spoils, a pretty generous tip, but the king of Sodom refused his take, saying, "Just give me the people and you keep the loot."

Abram replied, "I swear by God Most High, creator of heaven and earth, that I just want my expenses covered."

Chapter 15

Yahweh Makes a Deal with Abram

Sometime later, Yahweh spoke to Abram in a vision: "Fear not, Abram. I got your back."

"You got my back? Well, how about giving me a son then, you prick! As is, I'll have to pick some dope from my household to be my heir."

"No, your heir will be your son!"

Yahweh took Abram outside (I'm not sure how a vision takes you outside, but okay) and showed him all the stars in the sky. "Count 'em, if you can. Your descendants will number the stars in the sky."

Abram could only count about three thousand stars and this may have been a bummer, but he was satisfied and he believed in Yahweh, who told him, "I am Yahweh who brought you out of Ur of the Chaldeans and I give you this country as a gift."

Again.

Then Abram had the temerity to ask, "How do I know it's true? I mean, you're only going to give me three thousand descendants. How do I know I can trust you?"

"Bring me a three-year-old heifer, a three-year-old she-goat, a three-year-old ram, a turtle dove and a young pigeon."

It was some ridiculous order, but Abram collected and split the animals, but not the birds, down the middle and laid them all out, I guess on the ground, and then he spent the day shooing vultures away from this putrid, idiotic mess.

Then, as the sun set, Abram fell into a trance and a deep, dark dread descended on him, and go ahead and imagine Bob Dylan singing.

Yahweh appeared and promised Abram, "You will have a great life and a peaceful death, but wait till you see how I fuck your descendants! They'll be miserable slaves for 400 years. Only then will I judge their masters and free them with fabulous prizes."

Kind of a mixed blessing, huh?

Have a great life, but your grandchildren will live in hell for 400 years for absolutely no reason!

Yahweh added, "They will return in the fourth generation, for until then the iniquity of the Amorites will not have peaked."

Oh, so that's it! The fucking Amorites—should have known. And, remember, back then a generation was a hundred years and women did not have children until they were at least 90 years old, so just play along if you're doing the math.

The sun set, darkness came, a smoking firepot appeared and a flaming torch passed among the disgusting mess of animal parts on the ground and I have no idea what all this nonsense is about, but it apparently heralds a very special moment.

Yahweh gives Abram Canaan, again

Yahweh promised Abram, "I give your descendants the country from the Great River of Egypt to the Euphrates River and all the people in it, including the Canaanites."

Well, I thought it would be special, but it turns out that Yahweh just gave Abram Canaan, for what? The fourth? Fifth time?

I've lost count.

Chapter 16

Abram Fucks Sarai's Slave

Abram and Sarai remained childless.

"Look," Sarai finally said to Abram. "Yahweh won't give me children, so why don't you fuck my slave-girl, Hagar? Maybe I'll get a child through her."

Just fuck my slave-girl!

What a simple solution to the problem! I can't believe Planned Parenthood hasn't adopted it for today's god-cursed infertile couples.

Abraham, I guess with a straight face, perhaps feigning reluctance, agreed to fuck Hagar all right, and when she got pregnant, she got uppity and this pissed Sarai off.

She stomped over to Abram and said, "Now that she's pregnant, that little slave-bitch is a pain in my ass!"

"Well, she's just a slave," Abram replied. "Treat her any way you want."

Sarai treated Hagar so badly that the poor, pregnant slave-girl ran off into the desert and Yahweh appeared to her by a spring on the road to Shur.

"Hagar, Sarai's slave-girl, what in hell are you doing?" Yahweh asked.

"I'm running away from my mistress!"

"Go back to your mistress and kiss her ass!" Yahweh said. "You will have a son that you must name Ishmael, for I understand your distress. He will be a defiant wild man, but I will give him countless descendants and some of them will explode in restaurants and on school buses."

Hagar gave Yahweh the name "El Roi" because she was astounded to see him and live. She turned right around, ran back to Sarai and she gave birth to Ishmael when Abram was 86 years old.

Chapter 17

Yahweh Makes the Same Deal with Abram Again

When Abram was 99 years old, Yahweh appeared to him and said, "I am El Shaddai (Mountain God). Behave yourself and I'll give you many descendants."

Abram bowed to the ground.

God changes Abram's name to Abraham and makes the guys skin their dicks

And God (suddenly he's "God," not Yahweh or El Shaddai) said to him, "I'm changing your name to Abraham because you will father many nations, your sons will be kings, I will be your god and their god, and I give you Canaan, forever! All you guys have to do is skin your dicks and your newborn boys' dicks when they are eight days old, and this applies to your slaves as well. Any guy without a skinned dick is out the club!"

What?

You heard me! God just made Abraham patriarch of the Judeo/Christian/Muslim world and gave him Canaan and promised to be their god and all he wants is for the guys to skin their dicks! I understand you're dumbfounded, but I'm just telling you what the Bible says.

Then God added, "And as for your wife Sarai, I'm changing her name to Sarah and I will give her a son and she will be the mother of kings and nations."

Abraham bowed low and laughed, thinking, "I'm a hundred years old, Sarah is ninety, and we're going to have a son? What kind of nonsense is this?"

But he replied, just to appease God, "It's OK, I have Ishmael; it's enough."

But God was rolling, "No, Sarah will give you a boy named Isaac and I will be his god and both he and Ishmael will father great nations and all you guys have to do is skin your dicks!"

Well, all right...

At age 99, Abraham skinned his dick, then Ishmael's, and then he skinned the dicks of all his men, including his slaves, and I know what you're thinking: Abraham, the patriarch of the Judeo/Christian/Muslim world, had slaves?

Yup!

The Bible is fine with slavery, accepts it as a normal and completely acceptable aspect of life and never, I mean no one in the Bible—not God, not Abraham, not Moses, not even Jesus—ever once condemns it!

Huh?

Get used to it.

Chapter 18

Yahweh has Lunch with Abraham

Abraham was sitting outside his tent by the Oak of Mamre, when Yahweh walked up with two buddies.

Abraham leaped up to greet them.

Bowing low, he said, "My lord, please stop and wash your feet and rest under the tree. I'll buy you lunch and you can rest before continuing on."

Yahweh and his buddies accepted.

Abraham ran into the tent and gasped, "Sarah, quick! Knead three measures of your best flour and bake loaves!"

Then he ran out to the herd and grabbed a fine, tender calf and ordered his servant to cook it.

Meanwhile, I guess Yahweh and his buddies washed their feet and lounged in the shade of the oak tree, maybe impatiently, who knows, but whatever they did and however impatiently they were doing it, eventually curds, milk and roast calf were laid out before them and Abraham watched from the shade of the oak tree as they ate.

After a while, Yahweh asked Abraham, "Where is your wife?"

"She's in the tent."

Yahweh casually remarked, "I'll come back next year and give her a son."

Inside the tent, Sarah, who could not remember her last period, heard this and thought, "We're old as dirt and I'm going to get pregnant?"

And she pissed her pants laughing...

Yahweh heard her. "Why is Sarah laughing?" he asked, adding, "Nothing is impossible for me! I'll be back next year and you'll have a son!"

Abraham did not tell Yahweh that God had promised him a son in the last chapter.

Then Sarah appeared in the tent entrance, piss dripping down her leg. "I did not laugh," she lied.

But Yahweh was too sharp for her. "Oh yes you did!" he said.

It was a small thing, nothing further was said, and after lunch, Yahweh and his two buddies continued on their way to Sodom, Abraham in tow and Yahweh had a dilemma: He would make Abraham into a great nation. Should he tell him what he was about to do in Sodom or not?

Yahweh and Abraham on the road to Sodom

They walked along.

As they approached Sodom, Yahweh, apparently for Abraham's benefit, said, "I've heard that Sodom is overrun by fudge packers. I'll go down and see for myself."

Except Yahweh did not; he sent his two buddies down into the city instead and he stayed behind with Abraham.

Abraham guessed what Yahweh was up to and worked up the courage to speak, "Suppose there are 50 straight men in the city. Will you destroy them with the butt fuckers?"

Yahweh replied, "If I find 50 straight guys in Sodom, I will spare the city."

"Look, I don't mean to be a pain in the ass," Abraham said, "but what if there are only 45 straight guys? Will you destroy the city for the lack of just five straight guys?"

"Well, all right. If I find 45 straight guys in Sodom, I will spare the city."

Emboldened, Abraham began working Yahweh. "What if there are only 40 straight guys in Sodom?"

"I will spare Sodom for 40 straight guys."

"30?"

"Alright, for 30."

"20?"

"Yes, OK."

"10?"

"All right, all right! If I find 10 straight men in Sodom, I will spare the city, but that's it!"

Yahweh left then; I don't know if he went into the city or back up into the sky or what, the Bible doesn't say, but it does say that Abraham turned around and went home.

Chapter 19

Yahweh Destroys Sodom

Yahweh's two buddies turn out to be angels and Abraham's nephew Lot greeted them deferentially at the city's gate, and don't ask me how he knew they were coming.

"My lords," Lot said to them. "Please come to my house and wash your feet and spend the night."

"Thanks, but we'll spend the night here in the Square."

"No, please!" Lot stammered. "Please come to my house! Please! I'm begging you! You must come to my house!"

"All right! All right! Calm down, we'll come to your house."

Lot brought the angels home and I guess he washed their feet and I know he fed them unleavened bread—every angel's dream, but as they prepared to retire for the night, suddenly they heard vile commotion outside Lot's house and peeked through a window.

All Sodom's men surrounded it, homosexually frenzied, panting and loosening their tunics.

"Grease your friends up and send them out!"

"We want to rape them!"

It was not the traditional Chamber of Commerce welcome.

"Hurry, it's my bowling night!"

Lot offers his virgin daughters for a no-holes-barred gang bang

Lot appeared on his doorstep.

"Please brothers, don't be wicked!" he begged them. "Look! I have two beautiful virgin daughters! Take them and fuck them any way you want! Any hole you want! As many times as you want! Only please, I beg you to spare my guests!"

A magnanimous offer and one not often repeated in human history, I'm sure, and also one the Bible has no problem with. You get the feeling that if the men had calmed down and replied, "Well all right, give us your virgin daughters and we'll gang rape them instead," the Bible would have been fine with it.

But this mob wanted nothing to do with pretty young girls.

"No disgusting girls!" they cried, and the Sodomites rushed Lot, knocked him aside, and banged on his door!

Suddenly it opened and the angels grabbed Lot, ripped him back into the house and slammed the door shut! Then they blinded the Sodomites with a light so brilliant they could not see the door.

Back inside, the angels told Lot that Yahweh sent them to destroy Sodom and he better get his ass and those of his family out of town fast!

Lot burst out the door.

Don't ask me what became of the blinded butt fuckers—I guess they were stumbling around, screaming, crashing into things, and maybe Lot elbowed his way through them, I don't know, the Bible doesn't say. It just says that Lot ran and found his future sons-in-law and when he found them, he did not admit to offering their fiancées for a no-holes-barred gang bang, he just breathlessly explained that Yahweh was going to destroy the city and they should run for their lives!

But the boys just laughed at him, and I guess Lot limped back home, perplexed and disappointed.

Meanwhile, the night passed.

At daybreak, the angels told Lot, "Now get your family out of town before all hell breaks loose!"

When Lot hesitated, demonstrating Yahweh's mercy, the angels grabbed him and his family and dragged them through the streets of Sodom, out to the edge of town.

"Now run for your lives!" the angels yelled. "And whatever you do, don't look behind you and don't stop! Run for the hills or you will be annihilated!"

"My lord! You've been great to me and you saved my life and all, but if I run to the hills, I will die!" Lot replied idiotically. "Could we just, you know, run over to that little town over there?" He pointed it out. "It's a small place, but we'll be fine there."

"All right, all right! Go there and I promise we will not destroy it, but we can't do anything until you get there, so hurry!"

For that, the town was named Zoar.

Yahweh turns Lot's wife into a pillar of salt

The angels waited patiently while Lot and his family ran for the little town. The sun was just rising as they stepped into it and as soon as they did, Yahweh began raining fire and brimstone down on Sodom and Gomorrah and the surrounding plain! It was loud and terrifying like nothing ever seen or heard before and Lot's wife, seeing the fire and brimstone raining down from the sky, hearing the tortured screams behind them, well, she couldn't resist taking one quick look back...

Flash!

Just like that, Yahweh turned her into a pillar of salt. That's right, a pillar of goddamned salt!

Kind of a strange choice, if you ask me. Couldn't Yahweh have turned her into something a little more useful? Like a chair or a shovel? I'm not sure what turning Lot's wife into a pillar of salt says about the guy, but I won't dwell on it and the Bible does not record Lot's reaction to his wife becoming a pillar of salt, but you don't think he maintained a loving relationship with her, do you? I mean, he didn't go out into the street and dry hump a pillar of salt, did he?

Well, who knows?

Abraham watches Sodom and Gomorrah smolder

The next morning, back at the scenic overlook he had shared with Yahweh the day before, Abraham stood and watched smoke rising from the ashes of Sodom and Gomorrah, and don't ask me why God did not turn him into a pillar of salt; I guess that curse had expired. God had destroyed the cities and protected Abraham and Lot, but get this: As soon as the dust settled on the remains of Sodom and Gomorrah, Lot moved up into a cave in the very same hill country he had predicted would kill him.

Go figure!

Lot gets drunk and fucks both his daughters

There, of course, Lot's two virgin daughters had this dilemma: Yahweh had incinerated their fiancés and now they lived in a cave in the boondocks with no prospects for motherhood, but fear not! They were enterprising young girls and they got their father so drunk that he fucked them both and didn't remember it the next day. Lot may have subsequently wondered how in hell they both got pregnant and who the fathers might be, but the Bible doesn't say. Nine months later, his oldest daughter birthed Moab, ancestor of the Moabites and his youngest daughter birthed Ben-Ammi, ancestor of the Bene-Ammon.

And so the story ends happily with a drunk dad fucking and impregnating both his daughters and them birthing their own stepbrothers, but no one knows if the pillar of salt attended either birth.

Chapter 20

King Abimelech Almost Fucks Sarah

Abraham moved to the Negeb and settled between Kadesh and Shur. One day, he and Sarah visited Gerar where he of course introduced his wife as his "sister" and of course King Abimelech immediately had to fuck her. I guess she remained such a complete piece of ass at ninety that the king just had to have a little and, by the way, have you noticed that wherever Abraham goes he passes off Sarah as his sister and lets any available king fuck her to avoid having a bad day? A little insight into the character of the patriarch of the Judeo/Christian/Islamic world!

Anyhow, Sarah was now in the king's harem in line to be fucked, but before Abimelech got to her, God appeared to him and said, "I must kill you, because you are about to fuck a married woman!"

Abimelech, somehow knowing he meant Sarah, did not understand. He had not even felt Sarah up yet and God wanted to kill him?

"Lord," he protested. "Why kill an honest man? He said she was his sister. She said he was her brother. How am I to blame?"

"I know," God replied. "That's why I stopped you from fucking her."

Did I get this right?

God wants to kill Abimelech for planning to fuck a secretly-married ninety-year-old woman that he, God, has prevented him from fucking?

Is that it?

Well, it doesn't really matter, because now God changed his mind.

"On second thought, forget that and send Abraham's wife back to him because he's a useful prophet, and if you don't send her back, I will kill you and all your family."

Nice of God to include the family.

The next morning, Abimelech had Abraham dragged in before him.

"Why did you tell me your wife was your sister?" the king barked. "You had no right to treat me like this! Why did you do it?"

Abraham replied, "I thought no one here feared God and you would kill me and fuck my wife." Then he introduced a new twist, "Besides, she really is my sister! She's my father's daughter, but not my mother's, and when we travel, I tell her, 'If you love me, just say you're my sister.'"

King Abimelech should have said, "Are you out of your fucking mind? Why in hell would I kill you to fuck a 90-year-old broad?" But instead, he sent Sarah back to Abraham and rewarded him with sheep, cattle, and slaves.

"All my land is yours," said the king. "Settle anywhere you like!"

The King rewards Abraham for lying

Then the king told Sarah, "I'll give Abraham a thousand pieces of silver to eliminate all suspicion about you and prove your innocence."

And I know what you're wondering, why would the king reward Abraham for lying to him about his wife and almost getting him and his family killed by God?

Meanwhile God had rendered Abimelech's wife and all his slave-girls barren to punish him for almost fucking Sarah, but now Abraham somehow convinced God to restore their fertility.

Another happy ending to another ridiculous story.

Chapter 21

God finally gives Sarah a son and Abraham runs Hagar and Ishmael out of town

After many years and many promises, Yahweh finally allowed Sarah to get pregnant and have a son! Abraham named him Isaac and skinned his dick just like Yahweh wanted, and he and Sarah were delighted with their newborn baby boy.

Please understand what the Bible is saying here: A 100-year-old man's previously-barren, 90-year-old wife just gave birth to a baby and they couldn't be happier! Oh, and it's four thousand years ago, when human life expectancy was about 29 years. It's pure lunacy, but we'll play along, just like it actually happened.

Sarah said, "God made me so happy! Imagine, having a son at my age!"

When baby Isaac was weaned, Abraham hosted a banquet to celebrate the happy occasion and there's nothing better than a party hosted by a 100-year-old man, but as baby Isaac grew and became a little boy, it upset Sarah to watch him play with her slave's son, Ishmael.

So she cornered Abraham. "Get rid of that slave-bitch Hagar and her son!" she demanded. "I don't want that little prick Ishmael sharing Isaac's inheritance!"

This disturbed Abraham because Ishmael was also his son, so he consulted God.

"Fuck Ishmael and the slave-girl!" God advised him. "Obey Sarah because Isaac will carry on your name and don't worry, I'll make Ishmael into a great nation, too."

Abraham took God's advice.

The next morning, he gave Hagar some bread and a skin of water, threw Ishmael on her shoulder and before I go any further, I have to do the math. If Abraham was 86 at Ishmael's birth and he's 99 now, then Abraham just threw a thirteen-year-old boy onto his mother's shoulder? Was she now staggering off under the weight of a near fully-grown boy?

Well, of course not.

In this story, Ishmael remains an infant and this confusion is caused by the different source documents, so we'll disregard it and guess that Abraham stood and waved as Hagar carried his son Ishmael off into the desert of Beersheba. Don't ask me why she went there, but she did and the going was tough, and when they ran out of water, Hagar laid Ishmael down under a bush, not wanting to watch the little guy die, and she stumbled away and slumped down, exhausted, and began sobbing.

God promises to make Ishmael a great nation

God heard Ishmael crying under the bush and called down from heaven. "Don't worry, Hagar. I hear the boy crying. Go pick him up and hold him, for I am going to make him a great nation."

Hagar went and picked up Ishmael and suddenly a well of cool, sweet water appeared and Hagar filled her skin with water and gave Ishmael a drink.

The Bible does not offer much subsequent detail here, but it appears that Hagar and Ishmael lived on in the desert of Paran thereafter and Ishmael grew up and became an archer and Hagar eventually went to Egypt and got him a wife.

That's all we're told.

King Abimelech and Phicol confront Abraham

Meanwhile, about this time, King Abimelech and Phicol, the commander of his army, arrived and confronted Abraham. "Since you're God's favorite," the king said, "swear to me that you will never fuck us and that you will treat us with the same love that I have always shown you as a guest in my land."

"I swear it," Abraham replied. "But I do have a small problem with you. Some of your servants stole a well from me."

"I had no idea!" Abimelech replied. "You never mentioned it before."

Abraham then presented Abimelech with some sheep and cattle, they made a covenant and Abraham put seven lambs off to the side.

"What in hell are you doing?" Abimelech asked,

"You must accept these lambs as evidence that I dug this well."

I'm not sure how this works. Abimelech's guys seized Abraham's well and now Abraham is paying him to prove that he dug it? Well, that's what the Bible says and it's not worth arguing.

Abimelech accepted the lambs and the place was named Beersheba because of the oath sworn there, even though it was already called Beersheba in the previous story.

Abimelech and Phicol left and Abraham planted a tamarisk at Beersheba and invoked the name of Yahweh there and Abraham lived in the land of the Philistines for a long time.

Chapter 22

God orders Abraham to incincrate his son

God called out, "Abraham!"

"I'm right here."

"Take your beloved son Isaac to a mountain I will show you in the land of Moriah and sacrifice him on an altar to me."

This could not have made Abraham happy. Here he had waited a hundred years for Isaac's birth and now God wanted him to incinerate him! But he dutifully chopped up some firewood, saddled his donkey, grabbed Isaac and a couple servants, and they set off for the land of Moriah, travelling three days until they saw the mountain that I guess God pointed out.

They made their way to the base of the mountain and Abraham told his servants, "Stay here with the donkey while Isaac and I go up the mountain to worship."

Little Isaac carried the firewood and Abraham carried the fire and the knife. As they made their way, little Isaac asked innocently, "Father, we have the fire and the wood, but where is the sacrificial lamb?"

Now that's gotta break your heart. You're taking your boy up a mountain to incinerate him and the poor kid asks that.

"Don't worry, son." Abraham replied. "God will provide the lamb for the burnt offering."

When they arrived at God's specified place, Abraham built an altar there and arranged the firewood under it, and then he bound little Isaac and laid him on the altar.

There was no "Dad! What are you doing?" or anything like that, the Bible simply states what Abraham did.

Then Abraham raised his knife over his head, ready to plunge it down into his little boy's heart.

Just then, Yahweh called down from the sky, "Abraham! Abraham!"

"What?" Abraham was torn from his trance. "I was about to sacrifice my boy! Now what?"

God spares Isaac and promises to make Abraham great

"Do not kill the boy! I was just testing your love for me."

Then Abraham saw a ram caught by its horns in a nearby bush and he untangled it, stabbed it to death, dragged it over to the altar, and incinerated it as an offering to Yahweh.

He named the place "Yahweh provides," hence today's saying, "On the mountain, Yahweh provides." Though I've never heard anyone say it.

Now Yahweh called down to Abraham from heaven again: "I swear by myself that because you would incinerate your beloved son for me, I will shower you with blessings and make your descendants as many as the stars of heaven and the grains of sand by the sea. Your descendants will rule the earth because you obeyed me today!"

I guess we're still waiting for that promise to materialize.

Anyhow, Abraham took Isaac back down to the servants and they all returned to Beersheba and settled there and eventually Abraham learned that his brother Nahor's wife and concubine had both borne him children and their meaningless names are listed here to end this ridiculous chapter.

Chapter 23

Sarah Dies

Sarah lived 127 years and died among the Hittites, at Kiriath-Arba, now Hebron, in Canaan, presumably still a piece of ass.

Abraham knelt by her and mourned.

When he finally looked up, he asked the Hittites, "I know I'm a stranger, but may I please buy a decent tomb for my wife?"

"Any goddamn tomb you want!" they replied. "Pick from our finest, no one of us will refuse you his tomb for your dead wife."

Abraham rose and bowed low.

"I'd like the cave at the edge of the field that Ephron son of Zohar owns at Machpelah," he said, adding, "I'll pay full price."

Ephron son of Zohar emerged. "It's yours, no charge! Witnessed by all my relatives! Please, go and bury your dead."

Abraham bowed low. "Ephron, please allow me to pay the full price for your field and I will bury my wife in the cave there."

"Fine, pay me 400 silver shekels if you want, who cares? Go and bury your wife."

Abraham pays retail for a grave

The local Hittites watched Abraham weigh out 400 shekels worth of silver and give it to Ephron, violating what would one day become the accepted Jewish tradition of never paying retail, but no matter. Abraham now owned a fine burial site for himself and his wife.

Chapter 24

Isaac Marries Rebekah

Abraham grew very old and he was blessed by Yahweh.

"Place your hand under my thigh," he said to his headman, "and swear by Yahweh that you will not choose a Canaanite wife for my son. Go to my homeland and find one of my relatives to marry Isaac."

He did not add, "Because you know how effective inbreeding is when forming a Royal Family."

And his headman did not say, "Are you out of your fucking mind, place my hand under your thigh? What kind of gay move is that?"

He simply said, "What if she won't come back to Canaan with me? Should I bring her back to Isaac or what?"

"No!" Abraham was adamant. "Yahweh brought me here and gave me Canaan for my descendants! If she refuses to return with you, so be it, but do not take my son to her, that you absolutely do not do!"

The headman placed his hand under Abraham's thigh (go ahead and cringe), swore it, and then he loaded up ten camels with prizes and set out for the city of Nahor in Aram Naharaim.

The Bible does not narrate the trip; whether it took a day or two or a week, I don't know, but when he arrived with the ten prize-laden camels, it was evening and he parked them down by a spring outside of town, at the time when young women came out from town to draw water.

The headman prayed to Yahweh, "God of my master, Abraham, show him you love him! I'll wait here until the young broads come out for water. I'll ask one, 'Please lower your pitcher and give me a drink.' If she is the one, make her say, 'Drink all you want and I'll water your camels too.'"

Yahweh apparently agreed to this way-too-complicated plan and the headman had barely finished his preposterous prayer when Abraham's niece, Rebekah, emerged from town with an empty jug on her shoulder. She was an absolutely beautiful, unspoiled virgin and the headman watched her ass wiggle down to the spring. She filled her jug, shouldered it, and came back up the bank.

The headman intercepted her and asked, "May I please have a drink of water?"

"Sure." Rebekah lowered and offered her jug. "Drink all you want." Then she sealed the deal, "And when you're finished, I'll water your camels too."

The Bible does not say if heavenly music played now or not, but if it didn't, it should have, and in the movie version, it certainly will. When the headman finished drinking, Rebekah emptied her jug into a convenient trough, ran back down for more water, and never mind that the camels could simply go down and drink from the spring, why ruin a good story?

The headman watched the beautiful girl water the camels, wondering if this was all Yahweh's doing. When she finished, certain now that she was the one, he put a half-shekel gold ring in her nose and slapped a five-shekel gold bracelet on each of her wrists and it was all fine with her.

The headman got right to the point, "Please tell me, who is your father and can we spend the night at his house?"

Quite a leap from requesting a drink of water, but the beautiful, newly-ringed and braceleted girl simply replied, "I'm Bethuel's daughter. Nahor and Milcah are my grandparents and we have plenty of straw and fodder and room for you to spend the night."

The headman bowed low and thanked Yahweh for leading him straight to his master's brother's house.

Rebekah ran straight home, rings jangling, and joyously announced her engagement! Strange for a girl to engage herself to a complete stranger after a five-minute talk with another stranger, but I won't contest this stupidity.

As soon as he heard her story, Rebekah's brother Laban ran out and found Abraham's headman. "You are blessed by Yahweh!" he gushed. "Come, we have room for all of you and your camels at our house."

So the headman and his companions followed Laban home. Laban helped unload the prizes and accommodated the men and the camels.

Then he took the headman inside and introduced him to his family: "This is Uncle Abraham's headman."

"Glad to meet you!"

"How about something to eat?"

"I cannot eat until I speak."

"Then speak."

"I am Abraham's servant. Yahweh, who once had lunch with my master, made him rich and he is leaving everything to his son, Isaac, but he does not want Isaac to marry some Canaanite pig, so I came here to find a wife for him. Yahweh chose Rebekah for Isaac and he will bless this marriage, so I decorated her with gold and, what do you say? Do you agree to this marriage or not?"

"Yahweh decided for us," they replied. "Take Rebekah back with you and she will marry Isaac as Yahweh decreed!"

Well, that was one hell of a half hour in a young woman's life!

Abraham's headman bowed low before Yahweh. Then he passed out the prizes and they all ate and drank and celebrated into the night.

The next morning, the headman said, "I'd like to return to my master now."

Laban and his mother replied, "Let Rebekah stay with us for ten more days and then she can go."

"I can't be delayed; I want to give my master the good news as soon as possible."

"Well, we'll ask the girl."

They found Rebekah and asked her.

"Are you kidding?" she replied. "I got enough gold in my nose to buy this whole goddamned town! Of course I'll go!"

And so her family blessed the marriage. Her sisters even said, "May tens of thousands spring from you and conquer their enemies!"

Then Rebekah, her nurse and her maids mounted camels and the little caravan headed off for Canaan.

Meanwhile Isaac was back from the well of Lahai Roi and living in the Negeb when he saw the little caravan approaching.

As soon as she saw him, Rebekah jumped down from her camel and asked the headman, "Who is that man approaching us in the fields?"

"He is my master."

Rebekah veiled her face.

Isaac arrived.

The headman told him the whole story.

Isaac's dick started doing jumping jacks and he dragged sweet, young Rebekah directly back to his tent and "made her his wife."

I guess it was a short courtship and a fairly simple ceremony in those days. And Isaac's love for Rebekah helped him deal with his mother's death.

Chapter 25

Abraham remarries, has six more kids, and then actually dies

The last chapter may have you believing that Abraham had grown very old, was near death, and only wanted to see Isaac marry before he died.

But, not quite.

Because now that young, barely 137 years old prick leaped out of his supposed deathbed and married a young broad named Keturah and she bore him six, count 'em, six more children! The only memorable one being Midian, but all of them and many of their descendants are listed here by names I won't bore you with.

And, of course, throughout his life Abraham had concubines for sport-fucking and they spit out illegitimate sons that he paid off and sent to the "Land of the East" to spare Isaac from them, and it's doubtful he cared enough about his illegitimate daughters to even bother naming them.

When Abraham finally died at the age of 175, I'm sure they pounded his chest, and shook and kicked him, and pried open his eyes, and yelled, "Is the son of a bitch actually dead?"

"I don't believe it!"

"Kick him again! I think I saw him blink!"

"Watch out! He'll jump up and marry another young broad!"

But he did not.

Abraham finally, actually died and was "gathered to his people," and the prick left every goddamned shekel to

Isaac, as promised, fucking Ishmael and all his other children.

Fucked or not, Ishmael was good enough to help Isaac entomb Abraham next to his first wife Sarah in the cave Abraham bought from the Hittites.

Ishmael and Isaac

Ishmael:

The story of Ishmael is short and sweet. He lived in the territory of Hailah-by-Shur, just outside of Egypt, had twelve sons (of course) and certainly some unnamed daughters, and he died at the age of 137. The Bible doesn't care much about Ishmael, see the Koran for more info.

Isaac:

God blessed Isaac and he settled near the well of Lahai Roi and married Rebekah when he was forty years old and she (of course) was barren until Isaac prayed so hard that Yahweh finally relented and let her conceive twins.

Her pregnancy was so difficult that she finally consulted Yahweh about it. The Bible does not characterize this consultation, but I've noticed that Yahweh does not walk around on the earth like he used to, and I suspect that it was long distance, but however Rebekah conversed with Yahweh, it went like this:

"It's like there's a fight in my belly and it's driving me nuts!"

"You have the fathers of two nations in your belly and the younger will subdue the older."

It was a short consultation, but I'm sure it made Rebekah feel much better.

Isaac was 60 years old, a little young by biblical standards, when Rebekah finally gave birth to the twins. His firstborn was a hairy redhead he named Esau and the second-born was dragged out of Rebekah holding onto Esau's heel, so they named him Jacob. Esau became Isaac's favorite because he grew up to be a strong hunter, but Rebekah preferred Jacob, who was more of a mama's boy.

Esau sells his birthright for a mouthful of stew

One day, Esau returned from a hunt exhausted and hungry and saw that Jacob had cooked up some lentil stew.

"Hey," Esau asked Jacob, "can I have one mouthful of your stew?"

"Sure," Jacob replied, and with a straight face, he added, "But it will cost you your birthright."

What?

That's right, Jacob wants to charge his twin brother his birthright for one lousy mouthful of his crap stew. Remember, a birthright was everything for a firstborn son 4,000 years ago, entitling him to inherit 100 percent of his father's estate and no other son got a goddamned thing!

But Esau didn't give a rat's ass about his birthright. "I'm starving to death," he said. "What good is my birthright to me?"

Not exactly a long-term thinker, to be sure.

"Swear that you will give me your birthright!" Jacob said.

"I swear I will give you my birthright! Now how about some stew?"

Jacob gave his brother Esau some bread and stew in return for his firstborn birthright. I like to think that he was generous enough to give Esau more than one mouthful, but who knows, the Bible doesn't say, and Esau ate, drank and got up and left.

That was all he cared about a lousy birthright.

Chapter 26

Isaac in Gerar

A new famine began.

Yahweh appeared to Isaac and said, "Do not go down to Egypt; stay where you are. I'll keep my oath to your father to bless you and give you millions of descendants and all the nations on earth will kiss their asses, all because your father Abraham obeyed me."

Where Isaac was or stayed or went is very confusing here, so we'll just cut to the chase: When the narrative regains coherence, Isaac and Rebekah are in Gerar visiting king Abimelech, just like Abraham and Sarah once did.

Isaac claims his wife is his sister so guys won't kill him to fuck her

And just like his father before him, Isaac maintained that his beautiful wife was his sister, so the guys would just fuck her and not kill him. It's a recurring theme in Genesis, not a nice or an honorable one, but a recurring one, and all was well until Abimelech looked out his window one day and saw Isaac feeling Rebekah up in public.

Abimelech summoned Isaac immediately.

"I saw you feeling up Rebekah!" he cried. "She's not your sister; she must be your wife! How could you treat us like this?"

"I thought some guy might kill me to fuck her, so I said she's my sister!" Isaac blurted, carrying on the family tradition.

Abimelech replied, "What if one of us did fuck her? She's a piece of ass! It had to happen! Many of us could have fucked her and then what? We would be guilty as hell and all because of you!"

Isaac had no reply.

Abimelech sighed, shook his head in disbelief, and then ordered his people: "Anyone who touches either Isaac or his wife will be killed!"

Short and sweet.

After that, Isaac prospered in Gerar. He sowed his crops and Yahweh blessed him with a harvest one hundred times normal and kept right on blessing him. Isaac became so rich and successful that the Philistines began to envy him and you wonder: If Yahweh controls the harvests, why was there a famine in the first place? In fact, if he controls everything, why is there ever a problem with anything? The more you read, the more you conclude that this guy God is just a flat-out prick.

Anyhow, Abimelech eventually came to Isaac and said, "You must leave us, for you have become much more powerful than we are."

Isaac Re-digs Abraham's Wells

So Isaac moved his operation out to the Valley of Gerar, although it seems he was already there, but who knows or cares?

Isaac's father Abraham dug several wells in the Valley, but the Philistine herdsmen filled them with dirt and now Isaac had his men re-dig the wells and he gave them the same names that his father did.

Now I'm no desert nomad, but I'm thinking that if you are one, especially 4,000 years ago, why in hell would you fill up perfectly good desert wells with dirt? What's more precious in a desert than water? I'm willing to believe the Philistines were idiots, but even idiots would not fill up good desert wells with dirt.

Something's just not right here.

Anyhow...

When they finished re-digging all of Abraham's old wells, Isaac's men dug a new well. The herdsman of Gerar disputed it, claiming, "That water is ours!" Because they disputed this new well, Isaac named it Esek and I guess he abandoned it, I don't know, the Bible doesn't say.

It does say that he moved on and his guys dug another new well, but the Philistines claimed that one too, so he named it Sitnah and moved on.

His guys dug still another new well and this one was not disputed, so Isaac named it Rehoboth and said "Now Yahweh has made room for us to thrive in this country."

Except that he didn't stay in the country.

As soon as he finished digging this last well, he abandoned it and headed up to Beersheba and you wonder why in hell he spent all that time re-digging all the old wells and digging all the new wells and arguing with the Philistines about who owned them. I mean, it can't be real easy to dig a well by hand in the desert with what passed for a shovel in those days.

Could it? And this idiot, Isaac, abandons every well as soon as it's done? And when he finally does finish with all this nonsense, rather than settle and enjoy the fruits of his labor, he moves to Beersheba instead? Sure this is ridiculous, but I'll finish the story anyway.

Yahweh appeared to Isaac at Beersheba and said, "I am your father Abraham's god, but fear not, for I'm with you and I will bless you and multiply your descendants for Abraham's sake."

Isaac built an altar there and invoked the name of Yahweh, then he pitched his tent nearby and his servants dug yet another well.

Meanwhile, Abimelech unexpectedly arrived from Gerar with an adviser and Philcor, the commander of his army.

"What are you doing here?" Isaac asked him. "I thought you hated me?"

"It's obvious that Yahweh favors you," they replied (apparently three men speaking as one, perhaps singing, though I don't think the Bible ever breaks into a musical, but who knows?). Anyway, they continued, "We figured we'd better swear a treaty with you, so let us make a covenant that you will never harm us, because we never molested you and were always kind to you and let you go in peace, may Yahweh bless you!"

All this was fine with Isaac and he bought dinner and they all feasted and got drunk. Early the next morning they exchanged oaths, said farewell and parted friends.

That very same day, Isaac's servants told him they had struck water in a well they had been digging and Isaac named the well Sheba and the town is named Beersheba to this day...

Wait a goddamn minute!

Haven't we heard all this before?

Isaac already went to "Beersheba" earlier in this chapter. And back in Chapter 21, Hagar wandered the desert of "Beersheba" and Abraham swore an oath with Abimelech and Phicol at the same well and named the same place Beersheba to commemorate the oath they swore back then and...

What in hell is going on here?

Same Abraham well digging and confrontation with Abimelech story now applied to Isaac

Relax, it's a cute little literary trick that allows the Bible to repeat a story about Abraham and apply it to Isaac, is all. That's why the Philistines had to fill in the wells, so Isaac could dig the same wells and give them the same names that Abraham did.

Sometimes the Bible tries a little too hard, know what I mean?

This idiotic chapter ends with forty-year-old Esau marrying not one, but two Hittite women, Judith and Basemath, and this really pissed off Isaac and Rebekah, but no big deal is made of it.

Chapter 27

Jacob Steals Esau's Special Blessing

Isaac grew old and blind and one day he sent for Esau.
"Son!"
"I am here, Father."
"I'm very old, so go out and hunt some game and make me a delicious meal and I will give you my special blessing before I die."
"Yes, Sir!" Screwed out of his firstborn birthright, Esau leaped into action. Oh, boy! A special blessing!
Meanwhile, his mother overheard all this and decided that if anyone was going to get a special blessing, it was her favorite son Jacob, not that red-haired ape Esau! After all, Jacob had cheated Esau out of his birthright; why not cheat him out of his special blessing too? There's nothing like good, solid family planning and everyone can benefit from this biblical lesson.
While Esau was off hunting, Rebekah grabbed Jacob. "Look," she said to him, "Your father wants to give that sucker Esau a special blessing, but if we work fast, you can steal it from him! Here's the plan: Run out to the flock and grab a couple good, young kids. I'll cook them into a special meal, and you take it to your father and tell that old, blind bastard that you're Esau and he'll give you the special blessing."
"But Mother! Esau is hairy and I am not. If father touches me he will know I am cheating him!"
Notice that Jacob has no problem with the scam, he's just worried about pulling it off.

"Don't worry, the curse will be on me," Rebekah replied. "You just run and fetch the kids and leave the rest to me!"

Rebekah dresses Jacob up like an idiot

Jacob got the kids and Rebekah cooked them into a special meal for Isaac. Then she dressed Jacob in Esau's clothes, wrapped goatskins around his arms and neck, and handed him the steaming plate of lamb.

"Now, take this special meal to your father and steal that ape's—I mean Esau's—special blessing. Hurry, before he returns from the hunt!"

Imagine Jacob, the future patriarch of the Israelites, in ill-fitting clothes, neck and arms wrapped in goatskins, looking like a complete fucking idiot, arriving at his old, blind, brain-addled father's bedside with a phony "special meal" so he can steal his twin brother's special blessing.

"Father?"

Isaac opened his tired old eyes, tried to focus them, but could not. "Which son are you?" he asked weakly.

"I'm Esau, your first-born. I've brought your special meal."

Isaac was astonished. "How did you hunt and prepare it so fast?"

Jacob had a ready answer. "Your god Yahweh helped me."

Isaac remained skeptical. "Come closer so I can be sure you really are Esau, because you sound more like Jacob."

Jacob came close and Isaac touched him. "Well, you sound like Jacob, but you feel like Esau, though you're even hairy than I remember, you feel like a goddamned goat! But whoever you are, give me that special meal so I can eat."

Jacob served him the meal with wine and Isaac ate and drank until he was content.

Then, still not absolutely convinced, Isaac said, "Come closer and kiss me, my son."

Jacob embraced his father and kissed him and Isaac thought, "Well, he sounds like Jacob, but he feels like Esau and he smells like shit, so it must be Esau!"

Jacob preened in his ridiculous costume and Isaac blessed him: "May God give you heaven's dew, earth's riches, and all the grain and wine you can eat and drink! I curse anyone who curses you and I bless anyone who blesses you!"

Jacob said nothing; he had stolen his brother's blessing and he just turned and left, maybe peeling the goatskins off his arms and neck as he walked away, the Bible doesn't say.

Isaac realizes he's been had and gives Esau a second-rate blessing

But right after Jacob left, the real Esau arrived and happily announced, "Father! I'm here with your special meal!"

A bewildered Isaac asked, "What? What do you mean? Who is this?"

"It's me...Esau! Your first-born son!"

"What?" Isaac, suddenly realizing he'd been duped, trembled violently. "It must have been Jacob!" he cried. "I just finished eating what I thought was my special meal and I blessed the son-of-a-bitch and now he's blessed forever."

Esau was crushed. "Father, please! Bless me, too!" he cried.

"I can't son," Isaac wept. "Your conniving brother Jacob stole your blessing!"

"My blessing! He stole my birthright and now he has my blessing too!"

"That's right, son. You're fucked!"

"But Father, surely you can bless me too?"

When Isaac did not immediately reply, Esau began weeping.

"All right, all right, stop crying!" Isaac said. "Here's the best I can do for you: You don't get heaven's dew or earth's riches, and you'll live by your sword and serve your brother, but when you do win your freedom, you will shake his yoke off!"

Esau was incredulous at this bullshit, half-ass blessing and he hated Jacob for it and thought, "My father will die soon and then I will kill Jacob!"

Somehow Rebekah figured this out and told Jacob, "Esau is so pissed about you stealing his birthright and his special blessing that he will kill you after your father dies. Run to your Uncle Laban at Haran. Stay with him until Esau cools off and forgets that you fucked him. I'll send for you when it's safe for you to return."

"You mean like Michael going to Italy in *The Godfather*?"

"Yes, now go! I don't want to lose you and your father on the same day."

Then Rebekah went to her husband Isaac and complained, "Those two Hittite whores that Esau married make me wanna puke! If Jacob married even one such piece of Hittite shit, it would kill me!"

Chapter 28

Another version of Isaac blessing Jacob and sending him to Laban

This version of the story, obviously from a different source, does not require a deceitful, double-crossing wife and mother. Here Isaac simply summoned Jacob, blessed him, and said, "Do not marry a Canaanite woman! Go to your Uncle Laban in Paddan-Aram and choose a cousin for your wife and may El Shaddai give you Abraham's blessing so you can inherit Canaan, the country God gave to Abraham, where you now live as a stranger."

Of course, Abraham's blessing already gave Canaan to Jacob, but who cares?

Jacob left for Paddan-Aram in Haran and Esau, realizing his father hated Canaanite women, married his third—Ishmael's daughter Mahalath—I guess just to piss his father off.

Meanwhile, on his way to Haran, Jacob slept at Luz and dreamed he saw angels traversing a ladder between heaven and earth. In the dream, Yahweh said, "I am Abraham and Isaac's god. I give you and your descendants this land and everyone will kiss your asses, and I will always protect you and bring you back here."

When Jacob awoke, he thought, "Yahweh is here! This is truly God's place! It's the gate of heaven!"

He set his stone pillow up as a pillar, oiled it, renamed the place Bethel and vowed, "If God takes care of me until I get back home, Yahweh will be my god. This stone pillar will be a house of God and I will faithfully pay you a tenth of everything you give me."

Chapter 29

Jacob and Rachel

Jacob reached the Land of the Easterners and found three flocks of sheep lying around a well that was covered by a large stone.

He approached and asked the shepherds, "Why let the sheep lie around? Why not water them and then let them graze?"

Not one of them told Jacob to mind his own fucking business. They replied, "When the other shepherds arrive, we'll roll away the stone and water all the sheep."

They seemed like good enough guys, so Jacob asked, "Where you boys from?"

"Haran."

"Do you know Laban, son of Nahor?"

"Sure."

"Is he well?"

"Why not ask his daughter? Here she comes with his flock."

Jacob turned and when he saw Laban's beautiful daughter Rachel leading her father's sheep up to the well, he ran right over, rolled the stone away and watered her sheep.

Then he burst into tears, kissed Rachel, and blurted, "It's me, your cousin Jacob!"

"Well, goddamn! Cousin Jacob!"

Rachel ran right home with the great news, I guess leaving the sheep behind with Cousin Jacob—I mean, it's hard to run anywhere with a flock of sheep in tow, but the Bible doesn't say.

Back home, Laban received the news happily and ran out to the well. He kissed and embraced Jacob and brought him back home, I guess with all the sheep, and

Jacob updated everyone on all the family news back home, omitting how he stole Esau's firstborn birthright and special blessing.

Hearing it, Laban gushed, "You really are my flesh and blood!"

And just like that it was settled. Jacob moved into Laban's house and began working for him.

After a while, Laban said to him, "I know we're family, but I don't expect you to work for free, so how much shall I pay you?"

Laban had two daughters. Leah, the oldest, had lovely eyes, but she was ... well, let's be honest, she was a pig; but his youngest daughter Rachel was a complete piece of ass and Jacob was madly in love with her.

So he replied, "How about I work for you for seven years and then I marry Rachel?"

"Well, better you than some Hittite piece of shit," Laban laughed, slapping Jacob on the back. "It's a deal."

I don't know if Jacob sent word back home that he was living with Uncle Laban and working for him or not, the Bible doesn't say, but he worked those seven years and time flew by because he was so much in love with his beautiful Rachel. At last the great day finally came and Jacob ran and found Laban.

"Well, Uncle Laban, I have worked seven years for you as we agreed and now I'd like to marry Rachel."

"Of course, of course!" Laban patted him on the back and lied.

Laban tricks Jacob into marrying his pig daughter Leah

Laban gathered all his friends and family together for a great banquet to celebrate the wedding and it all seemed like a dream come true for Blue Balls—I mean, young

Jacob. But instead of the beautiful Rachel, Laban gave Jacob his pig daughter Leah instead, and somehow Jacob married her and everybody celebrated and then he fucked her all night, consummating the marriage without realizing she was not Rachel (and I understand this is somewhat implausible).

When Jacob woke the next morning and saw Leah cuddled up next to him, he leaped out of bed and ran screaming for Laban.

"What have you done to me?" he cried. "I worked my ass off for seven years for Rachel! Why did I wake up next to that pig, Leah?"

"Our custom is to marry off the oldest daughter first," Laban calmly replied. "But I'll tell you what, finish this marriage week and promise me seven more years of free labor and you can marry Rachel too."

Cosmic repayment for Jacob fucking Esau?

Who knows, the Bible doesn't say, and I'm sure Jacob was pissed, but he agreed to this ridiculous deal.

Jacob ends up with two wives

When Jacob's wedding week with Leah ended, Laban finally let him marry his beautiful daughter Rachel and now Jacob had two wives: one piece of ass and one pig. Jacob obviously preferred Rachel, and Yahweh, always on the job, saw that Leah was "unloved" so he unlocked her womb and let her get pregnant, while he kept sweet Rachel barren and childless in the tradition of all beautiful, important women in the Books of Moses.

Leah birthed a son she named Reuben, meaning "Yahweh saw my misery and now my husband will love me," and then she spit out three more sons in rapid succession: Simeon (Yahweh heard I was unloved and gave me this son too), Levi (now that I have three sons, my husband will love me) and Judah (now I shall praise Yahweh).

Then Leah stopped bearing children.

Chapter 30

Jacob fucks both his wives and both their slaves

Rachel kept score. Leah had four sons and she, none. It was no longer enough to be beautiful.

She went to Jacob and whined, "Give me children or I will die!"

"What, am I God?" he barked. "*He's* your problem, not me!"

Exasperated, Rachel went and dragged her slave-girl, Bilhah, back to Jacob.

"Here!" she cried. "Fuck my slave! I'll make her sit on my lap and give birth so her child will be mine."

An interesting concept, not especially practical, but interesting.

Now the Bible does not rate Bilhah as a piece of ass, but you gotta think this tempered Jacob's anger.

Fuck my slave!

"Well, all right, honey. If you insist..."

Jacob fucked Bilhah all right and knocked her right up and she gave birth to a son, apparently sitting on Rachel's lap, that Rachel stole and named Dan (God heard my prayer and gave me a son).

Jacob renews his slave-fucking license

Jacob kept right on banging Bilhah and she gave him a second son that Rachel stole and named Naphtali (I battled my sister and won), though she may have been a little quick with that naming, because now Leah decided that Jacob should fuck her slave-girl, Zilpah.

Jacob, ever the obedient husband, fluffed his dick up and pounded Zilpah and she gave him a son that Leah stole and named Gad (what good fortune) and then Zilpah gave him a second son that Leah stole and named Asher (women will call me blessed).

And have you noticed that all these biblical names translate into complete resumes? Hebrew is apparently a very efficient language.

Leah barters Rachel a sex romp with Jacob for narcotics

Sometime later, Reuben found some narcotic mandrake plants and gave them to his mother Leah. Rachel found out and cornered Leah.

"Hey, sister, you holding?"

"What?" Leah was indignant. "It's not enough that you stole my husband? You want my drugs too?"

"All right, I'll make you a deal. Give me a shekel bag and you can fuck our husband tonight."

Leah, probably remembering that she was, after all, a pig, relented.

"All right, it's a deal."

That night, Leah, probably all sexed up in goatskin lingerie, ran—I mean, waddled—out to greet Jacob when he came in from the pastures.

"I rented you from Rachel for the night!" she crowed. "You have to fuck me! Don't try to run!"

Who knows how enthusiastically, but Jacob honored the pig-sticking deal.

Meanwhile God, watching all this slave fucking, took pity on poor Leah and let her get pregnant again and she popped out a fresh son named Issachar (God rewarded me for letting my husband fuck my slave). Then she sneaked back into Jacob's bed and produced yet another son she named Zebulun (God gave me a fine gift for giving my husband six sons).

Then Leah got pregnant again—and you better sit down, because a biblical miracle occurred—this time she actually birthed a girl!

That's right, a GIRL!

G-I-R-L!

A girl is born!

A biblical rarity.

Leah named her Dinah and because she was a girl the name "Dinah" apparently meant absolutely nothing.

Now of course the biblical women gave birth to girls, but women are so insignificant in the Bible that one born is generally unworthy of mention. The Bible is all about men and generally ignores women, unless one is being fucked by her father or raped or something special like that. That said, let's get back to the baby birthing sweepstakes...

Guess what?

God finally answered Rachel's prayers! And don't ask me why he ever punished her in the first place. She was completely innocent and yet God struck her barren for all these years, while Leah and the slave-girls spat out sons like vending machines.

God finally lets Rachel have a son

But now God finally removed Rachel's disgrace and let her get pregnant! Halleluiah! Hire a chorus to sing it! Rachel had a son that she named Joseph and she was so happy, she cried, "Yahweh, give me another son!"

Meanwhile Jacob went to Laban and said, "Look, I've kept my word. I worked seven years for you for Rachel, not once, but twice, and I overlooked you tricking me into marrying that pig Leah, AND I made you rich! So please let me to take my wives and children and slaves and go."

Laban replied haughtily, "I know Yahweh blessed me because of you, so what do I owe you? Name your price."

"You know how hard I worked for you and how prosperous I made you. Yahweh has blessed you wherever I have been. When will I be able to provide for my own household, too?"

"I know, I get it! I understand! I'm asking, how much do you want? Just name it and I'll pay it!"

Jacob plots to rip Laban off

"Well, on second thought, you do not owe me any money and I will not leave; I will stay and tend your flock. All I ask is that you remove every black sheep and every spotted or speckled goat and give them to me as my wages. Then if you ever see me with a pure white animal, you'll know I stole it."

Laban, probably thinking, *"What kind of idiot is this?"* said with a straight face, "Deal!"

Laban cut the striped and speckled goats and black sheep out of his herds and gave them to Jacob and Laban's sons tended them for Jacob, while Jacob tended Laban's sheep.

Huh?

Why would Laban's sons (and he certainly had many) tend Jacob's little flock of irregulars, while Jacob alone tended Laban's great flocks of regulars? Shouldn't Laban's sons tend the great flocks he owns and Jacob tend his own little flock?

Of course, and another thing—anybody ever seen a striped goat? Didn't think so. What's going on here? This story is getting more preposterous by the second!

Just remember, it's a cartoon, nothing is real, anything can happen and get ready, because it's about to get a whole lot more ridiculous!

With the deal done and the flocks separated, Laban journeyed three days away and Jacob effected his secret plan. He peeled stripes into fresh poplar tree shoots and set them up near the watering spots where the goats came to drink and mate.

It was pure magic.

Goats mating in front of the stripes produced striped, spotted, and speckled kids, and don't ask me how the stripes produced the speckled and the spotted; this is all so ridiculous that I shouldn't even be repeating it, but I'm nothing if not true to the original. Then Jacob made sure the ewes faced something, anything black or striped or spotted when they mated, so they would produce black, striped and spotted kids.

And so Jacob got Uncle Laban's flocks to produce animals that he could add to his own flocks without having to steal them, obviously preferring good old fashioned cheating to outright theft. He then perfected his system by only allowing the healthiest animals to mate in front of the striped, spotted and the black things, while he left the sickly animals to their own devices.

Very generous of him!

Jacob eventually cheated his uncle out of enough animals to make himself very rich. Uncle Laban probably deserved it for that Leah-for-Rebekah swap bullshit, but let's stop and consider Jacob's herding technique in the service of his uncle. On the first level, it's ridiculous to think that animals that mate before striped things produce striped offspring, but then what isn't ridiculous in the Bible?

So we'll ignore that reality and just get basic.

Jacob's plan is immoral. He conspired to enrich himself with vast herds of strong, healthy animals at the expense of good, old Uncle Laban, who'll do just fine with the sickly animals Jacob left for him.

Well, what can you expect from a guy who stole both his twin brother's birthright and his special blessing?

I was going to ask you to draw your own conclusions here, but I'll save you the trouble: Jacob, the patriarch of the Jews—excepting Moses, perhaps the most important Israelite in the Torah—was a piece of shit!

Chapter 31

Jacob explains how he didn't rob Laban, that God gave him the animals, and goes home

Laban's sons eventually realized that Cousin Jacob had robbed their father blind and their relationship cooled.

Yahweh advised Jacob, "Better go home now, but don't worry, I got your back!"

Jacob called Rachel and Leah out to his pastures and explained to them, "Your father and brothers are pissed because they think I robbed them. You know how hard I worked for your father and how he fucked me, but God protected me. Your father paid me with spotted and striped animals. It's not my fault so many of them were born. I did not steal them from your father; God gave them to me!"

Only a true weasel would work God into his scam, now watch him roll...

"God gave me a dream. All the striped and spotted animals were mating, but the plain white animals were not, and God explained that he did this for me because your father screwed me. Then God told me, 'I am the god of Bethel, where you oiled a monument and vowed to me, and thanks again for the oil, but now I want you to leave this country and go home.'"

It was fine with the sisters.

"What's left for us here?"

"Our father treats us like foreigners, selling us like slaves and pissing away our inheritance."

"Surely all the riches God took from him and gave to you belong to our children, so obey God and go home!"

It was settled.

Jacob did not give notice. They just packed up, he threw his wives, children and slaves onto camels and the caravan set off for Canaan—a cocky Jacob thinking he had outsmarted Laban "the Aramaean" (and I don't know when he became "the Aramaean").

The little caravan crossed the river and headed for Mt. Gilead.

Laban rounds up his brothers and they chase down Jacob

Three days later, Laban realized they were gone with the stolen animals. He rounded up his brothers and they chased after them. A couple days later, they saw Jacob's caravan ahead at Mt. Gilead and stopped for the night.

That night God told Laban "the Aramaean" in a dream, "Do not say anything to Jacob!"

But the next day, as soon as he caught up to Jacob, Laban jumped off his camel, ran up and screamed at him, "How dare you outsmart me and carry off my daughters like prisoners of war? Fleeing in secret, not letting me kiss my daughters and grandchildren goodbye, when I would have sent you off with a celebration! You have behaved like a goddamned fool! I would kick your ass, but the god of your father told me not to say anything to you!"

Though he had just said plenty.

Laban accuses Jacob of stealing his gods

Then Laban added, "I know you got homesick and just wanted to go home, but why did you steal my gods?"

"Gods?" Jacob was astounded. "What gods? I was afraid you would not let me take your daughters, so I snuck out of town, but I didn't steal any gods! Search my people! I'll kill anybody you find with a god!"

Jacob was mightily offended, but what he didn't realize was that while everyone was busy packing, Rebekah had sneaked home and stolen her father's gods while he was off shearing his sheep.

Laban searched every tent but Rachel's, found nothing, and he entered Rachel's tent last. She was sitting on a cushion, Laban's gods hidden inside it, and said, "Forgive me for not standing, father, but it is my time of the month and I'm a bloody mess."

Laban rummaged about, finding nothing.

At this point, Jacob got pissed.

"What is my offense? Why are you hassling me? Have you found anything that belongs to you? If so, produce it now in the presence of your brothers and let them decide between us. I worked my ass off for you for years! Your ewes and she-goats never miscarried and I never ate your rams! I never brought a mauled animal back to you, I bore the loss myself, and you always made me pay. I suffered heat and frost! I never got a good night's sleep! You never changed! I worked fourteen years for your daughters and six years for your flock because you kept changing my deal. If Abraham's god had not been with me, I would have left with nothing! But God saw my plight and last night he delivered judgment."

"These are my daughters," Laban replied. "Their children are mine, the livestock is mine, everything you see is mine, but what can I do about it? So you and I will make a pact."

Jacob and Laban make a very confusing pact

Now get ready, because this is going to get real confusing:

Jacob set up a stone pillar as a memorial.

Jacob had his kinsmen collect stones and pile them into a cairn as a memorial.

Jacob called the cairn "Galeed" and Laban called it "Jegar-Sahadutha."

Laban said, "This cairn is a witness between us, so I name it Galeed, but we'll also call it Mizpah, because it lets Yahweh watch us when we can't see each other. If you treat my daughters badly or marry other women, remember God is the witness between us. I built this cairn and this pillar to mark our border. I will not cross to your side and you will not cross to my side to commit evil. May Abraham and Nahor's god judge us."

"I agree!" Jacob swore it by his ancestors' god. He offered a sacrifice and everybody enjoyed the meal and they all spent the night together on the mountain.

Here we actually have at least three versions of the story of how Jacob and Laban divided up the land and memorialized their agreement, all cut up and pasted badly together. Either Jacob or Laban set up a stone pillar or built a cairn and it was named either Galeed, Jegar-Sahadutha, or Mizpah. They're on Mt. Gilead. They're in the hills. God this, Yahweh that. I know it's a little confusing.

Get used to it.

Chapter 32

Jacob and Laban Part Company

The next morning Laban, his stolen gods apparently forgotten, kissed his daughters and grandchildren goodbye and headed home.

Jacob traveled in the opposite direction.

Along the way, he saw messengers of God and said, "This is God's camp," and he named the place Mahanaim.

Jacob sent word ahead to his brother Esau in Seir, the open country of Edom. "Tell him, it's me, Jacob! I've been staying with Laban, but I'm back now, I'm rich and I hope you are happy to see me."

Remember, Jacob had originally fled his homeland because Esau wanted to kill him and when Jacob's messengers returned and reported, "We saw your brother Esau. He's on his way to meet you with 400 men," the news scared Jacob shitless. He immediately divided his people and animals into two camps, thinking that if Esau attacked one camp, the other could escape.

Then Jacob said to Abraham and Isaac's god, Yahweh, "I left home with nothing but one lousy staff and now I'm rich! I don't deserve your love, but I beg you to protect me now from that hairy bastard Esau. I think he means to kill us all! Remember, you promised to protect me and give me countless descendants!"

That night, Jacob decided to send Esau two hundred she-goats, twenty he-goats, two hundred ewes, twenty rams, thirty camels in milk with their calves, forty cows, ten bulls, twenty female donkeys and ten male donkeys.

He ordered his servants, "Send these gifts ahead of me in separate droves. Have each drove leader tell Esau,

'We're from your brother Jacob. These animals are gifts for you and he is right behind us.'"

Jacob hoped the gifts would make Esau glad to see him.

Jacob wrestles God in the dirt and is renamed Israel

That night, Jacob sent everyone else across the Jabbok River and he stayed behind and camped alone, I guess by the river, and I understand this makes no sense.

Then "someone" appeared and they wrestled until dawn, possibly a no-holds-barred cage match, the Bible doesn't say, but when "someone" could not pin him, he punched Jacob's hip and dislocated it. But Jacob hung tough until "someone" finally yelled, "Let me go, it's daybreak!"

But Jacob held him tight and grunted, "I won't let you go until you bless me!"

"What is your name?"

"Jacob."

"You are no longer Jacob. Your new name is Israel because you prevailed against both God and men!"

"Not so fast!" Jacob grunted, still holding tight. "What's your name?"

"Why do you ask?"

Then "someone" blessed Jacob and must have disappeared, because suddenly he was gone,

Jacob named the place Peniel because, "I have seen God face-to-face and survived!" And to this day, the Israelites do not eat the thigh sinew from a hip socket, because God punched Jacob there.

Look, any reason to not eat sinew is a good one, but this preposterous story appears in the Bible for one simple reason: the source documents differ on who the patriarch of Judaism was. In at least one, it was Jacob and in at least one other, it was Israel. So this asinine story establishes Israel as the unambiguous patriarch of the Israelites.

As for the story itself—God's rolling around in the dirt, wrestling Jacob, and he can't even win?

God?

The all-powerful Creator and Ruler of the world can't defeat a mama's boy like Jacob in a wrestling match?

And after all the meetings with Jacob and all the great promises he made to him, God doesn't even know his name?

What kind of nonsense is this?

I'd say, complete.

Chapter 33

Jacob and Esau Reunite

(Remember, the Bible will now use the names Jacob and Israel to refer to the same guy, sometimes in the same paragraph, occasionally in the same sentence, so it can get confusing.)

Jacob saw Esau coming with four hundred men and quickly organized a welcoming committee. He placed the two slave-girls and their kids up front, followed by Leah and her kids, followed by Rachel and Joseph.

When Esau arrived with his men, Jacob ran up and bowed to the ground seven times to greet him. Esau (his plan to kill Jacob apparently forgotten) embraced Jacob and kissed him!

Then, noticing the women and children, Esau asked, "Who are they?"

"They are the children God gave me!" Jacob beamed proudly.

And his wives and their slaves brought all the children up to bow to Uncle Esau.

Then Esau asked, "What about all the gifts you sent me?"

"I wanted to make you happy."

"Brother, I have plenty!" Esau scoffed. "Keep what is yours."

But Jacob protested, "No, brother, please accept my gifts. It is like meeting God; you have received me so kindly. Accept my gifts, God has been good to me and I have plenty."

Esau reluctantly agreed to accept Jacob's gifts and said, "Come, let's break camp and travel together."

The reunion may not have been as happy as we thought, at least for Jacob, because he begged off. "As you can see, the children are weak, the calves slow us down, and I don't want to drive my herd too hard. You go ahead and I'll follow at a pace better-suited to the children and the herd. I'll catch up with you at Seir," he lied.

"At least let me leave some men to help you."

"What for? I have plenty of men. No, you just go on ahead and we'll be fine."

Esau shrugged and headed off for Seir with his 400 men, but Jacob did not follow him. He either built a house at Succoth or bought land outside of Shechem, pitched his tent and built an altar there he called "El, God of Israel," the Bible gets a little confused here.

Couple of things:

Obviously another two-version mash-up. Take your pick as to where Jacob actually settled and note that in neither version did he go on to Seir to meet Esau as promised.

The other thing is that "El" was the chief god of the Canaanites. Why build him an altar?

Chapter 34

Shechem Rapes Dinah and Then Asks to Marry Her

This story follows the source that settles Jacob outside of Shechem.

One day Jacob's daughter Dinah went out to visit some girlfriends. She was some piece of ass, strolling gaily along, when Shechem, son of Hamor the Hittite (the local headman), saw her.

His dick punched in!

Shechem stomped over, grabbed sweet, sashaying, unsuspecting young Dinah, ripped her clothes off, threw her down and raped her so furiously that stones cracked under her ass as he pounded her in the dirt! We're not told if Shechem raped Dinah in the road or in a ditch or in the shadow of a camel. We don't know where, or how many times he raped her, or how many people and/or camels watched him rape her, the Bible doesn't say, but we are told that by the time young Shechem had grunted and thrust and blown his last wad—I mean, seed—into sweet Dinah...

Why, that young rascal was in love!

He jumped up, tucked his dick in, and ran straight home. Bursting into his father's tent, he gushed. "Dad! I've found the girl of my dreams! I just fucked her in the road or in a ditch or in the shadow of a camel. I can't remember where or how many times or who was watching or if there were camels, I can't remember anything but that I love her and I have to marry her!"

You forget how tender young love can be.

Hamor grabbed his son by his shoulders. "Son!" he cried. "This is great news! I'll find this wonderful girl's father and we'll arrange the wedding immediately. I am, after all, the head man around here!"

"Gosh, dad! I hope so!"

And Father and son hugged, reveling in their good fortune.

Meanwhile Dinah limped back home, dripping, clothes all torn up, ass crusted with dirt and embedded with stones, and when Jacob saw her he realized she had been good and raped and he was pissed—really pissed! But he decided to restrain himself until his sons returned from the pastures, so he just sat in his tent, boiling in anger.

Guess who showed up?

Hamor the fucking Hittite shows up to negotiate the marriage

That's right, Hamor the fucking Hittite! Beaming like the sun! Happy as a freshly-watered camel!

Jacob received him with a certain reservation.

After the two men exchanged the customary pleasantries, Hamor got right to the point. "Jacob, my boy Shechem—he's a great kid, I promise you that! Anyhow, Shecky just raped your beautiful daughter in the road, or in a ditch, or in the shadow of a camel...," Hamor laughed, "The boy's so love-struck, he can't remember where! Anyhow, well my point is, these two lovebirds are meant for each other and I say, why wait? Let's marry them right now!"

Just then, Jacob's sons returned from the pastures.

"Boys," Jacob said coolly. "Meet Hamor the Hittite."

"Hamor the fucking Hittite?"

"That's right. His son Shechem just raped your sister Dinah in the road or in a ditch or the shadow of camel, we're not sure where, but he raped the shit out of her and now he wants to marry her!"

"This is an outrage!" the boys cried, infuriated. "An insult to Israel!"

"Now, boys..." Hamor tried to calm them. "Sure, my boy Shechem is a little impetuous, but he's heart set on marrying your beautiful sister. Tell you what, allow this marriage and our whole country and everything in it is yours for the asking. I'll give you anything you want, pay any price, just please let my son marry Dinah. He's a wonderful boy, and guess what?" Hamor grinned and threw open his hands. "He's right outside! I'll bring him in so you can meet him."

Incredibly, Hamor went outside and brought the lumbering, drooling, ungainly rapist into Jacob's tent.

"Gentlemen, I'd like you to meet my boy Shechem."

Shechem's knees were all scuffed up and dirty from pounding Dinah in the dirt, but he spoke politely, "Let me marry the girl and I'll give you anything you ask," he said. "Demand any bride-price you want and I will pay it. Only, please let me marry her! "

Jacob and his sons, at first astounded, then huddled for quite a while, talking it over. Finally, the sons gave Shechem a clever answer, "Sorry," they said, "but it would be disgraceful for us to give our sister to a man with a regular dick."

Shechem's spirit crashed.

Shechem can marry Dinah if the Hittite men skin their dicks

Until the boys added, "Unless, of course, you and all your men skin your dicks like we do! Do that and you can marry our sister."

Shechem exploded with joy! "Of course I'll skin my dick!" he cried. "We'll all skin our dicks! I love her so much, I'll skin goddamn anything! We all will! Right dad?"

Apparently dad agreed to a point where he just couldn't wait.

"Come Shechem," Hamor sang. "Let's go and announce the good news to our people!"

And just like that they were gone.

Jacob and his sons probably looked at each other in disbelief and asked, "How stupid are these guys?" But we don't know, the Bible doesn't say.

Meanwhile Hamor and Shechem quickly assembled all their men at the town gates and addressed them.

"These newcomers, Jacob and his people, they're fine men," Hamor began...

"Hey, Shechem!" Someone yelled from the crowd. "Why are your knees all scuffed up and dirty?"

Everyone laughed and Shechem blushed.

"All right, all right!" Hamor cried, quieting them. "As I was saying, these are fine men. Let them settle among us. There is plenty of room for everybody and we'll all be one big, happy family. And all they ask is that we skin our dicks!"

The men were stunned.

Finally, one cried, "Skin our dicks?"

"You mean, like a cucumber?"

"Are you out of your fucking mind?"

There was screaming and yelling and confusion.

"Quiet down, all of you!" Hamor the headman cried, settling them. "It's not as stupid as it sounds. They move in and smile and wave at us and we get all of their livestock! How's that for a deal? We're rich! And all we gotta do is skin our dicks!"

Well, when you put it that way...

It quickly became the greatest idea in the history of the world.

"Well, let's skin them then!" some guy yelled.

It's not clear how they did it—whether each man skinned his own dick or if they skinned each other's dicks or if one guy skinned all the dicks or what, the Bible doesn't say, and perhaps it's best left unsaid. All we know is that three days later, Shechem and Dinah were married and honeymooning at Shechem's place. I doubt there was much dancing at the wedding, what with all the men limping around in agony, holding their bloody crotches, and I won't even consider what Shechem's sore dick wedding night performance might have been like, but none of that mattered.

What did matter was that now the time was perfect.

Dinah's brothers slaughter all the sore dick Hittite men

After the wedding, Dinah's two full brothers, Simeon and Levi, sharpened up their swords, marched into town, and methodically and brutally slaughtered every limping, bloody crotch-holding, helpless piece of Hittite shit in town! They stabbed them! Repeatedly! And hacked off their heads and stomped them into pulp! And they chopped up Hamor and Shechem real extra special when they freed Dinah from her honeymoon nightmare!

Then the rest of Jacob's sons arrived at the massacre and they captured all the women, children, and cattle, and looted every house in town to avenge the rape of their sister.

But was Jacob happy when he heard what his sons had done?

Nope.

"You idiots!" he yelled at Simeon and Levi, Dinah's rape suddenly meaningless. "Now all the Canaanites and Perizzites will hate me and try to kill us all!"

"What?" the boys answered. "Should we just let them rape our sister like a whore?"

And so ends this heartwarming story of young love.

Chapter 35

Jacob Moves to Bethel and Deborah Dies

God told Jacob, "Move to Bethel and make me an altar there."

Jacob announced to his people, "Get rid of your foreign gods! Cleanse yourselves and change your clothes. We're moving to Bethel! I'll build an altar there for the best goddamn god there is!"

They gave Jacob all their foreign gods and earrings and he buried the crap under the oak tree near Shechem. When they broke camp, God scared the local Canaanites shitless so they would not pursue them, though it seems that only women and children would be left after the slaughter and why bother?

Jacob and company departed and soon arrived at Luz in Canaan. Jacob built an altar there and renamed the place El-Bethel, because God had appeared to him there when he fled Esau, and despite the fact that he had already arrived at Luz and built a monument there and renamed the place Bethel back in chapter 28.

Rebekah's nurse, Deborah, died in Bethel and they buried her under an oak tree and named it the "Oak of Tears."

El Shaddai changes Jacob's name to Israel, again, gives him Canaan, again, and Rachel dies

God appeared and blessed Jacob. "I am El Shaddai and I am changing your name to Israel because you will father many nations and your descendants will be kings. I give you the country I gave to Abraham and Isaac for all your descendants."

Of course, God had already changed Jacob's name to Israel after the famous wrestling match in chapter 32 and had already given the country to all Abraham's descendants, including Jacob, several times. There is no need to keep repeating the same stupid blessing over and over, but no matter.

After blessing Jacob, God rose up and disappeared into the sky and Jacob named the place El-Bethel (for at least the third time) because God spoke to him there, but they did not settle there as God ordered. They headed for Ephrath instead and Rachel died on the way, giving birth to a son she named Ben-Oni with her last breath. You might think a name given with a mother's last breath would be special, but no, as soon as she died, Jacob changed Ben-Oni's name to Benjamin.

Then Jacob buried his wife by the road to Ephrath, which is now Bethlehem, and raised a monument on her grave that remains today.

Reuben fucks his stepmother and Isaac dies

Israel moved on and camped beyond Migdal-Elder. There, Reuben fucked his brother Dan's mother and Israel found out, but took no immediate action.

Israel now had twelve sons from his two wives and their slaves and he went to Mamre at Kiriath-Arba, now Hebron, to visit his father Isaac, who was 180 years old.

Isaac died, was "gathered to his people," and Jacob and Esau buried him.

Chapter 36

Esau Founds Edom

Esau was also called Edom, probably so he could be credited with founding that nation, and he only married Canaanite women, three of them—Adah, Oholibamah, and Basemath—and don't ask me what happened to Judith and Mahalath.

Esau and Jacob's clans grew so big that there was no longer room for both of them in Canaan, so Esau moved to the mountains of Seir, and didn't he already live there when Jacob returned from Laban's place?

Well, whatever; Esau founded the nation of Edom and all of his immediate descendants are listed in this chapter as well as many of the kings of Edom that I won't bother naming.

Chapter 37

Joseph

Jacob settled in Canaan and his seventeen-year-old son Joseph, who tended Jacob's livestock with his brothers, informed his father that his brothers were lousy shepherds, so Jacob assigned Joseph to monitor them and rewarded him with a fancy tunic for being a rat.

One day Joseph recalled a dream to his brothers: "We were binding sheaves in the field and my sheaf suddenly rose upright and all your sheaves bowed down to it."

"So you're the king?" they scoffed. "Our lord, eh?" Joseph's brothers hated him for being the favorite son.

Then Joseph recalled another dream to his brothers and to his father in which the sun, the moon, and eleven stars (i.e., his father, mother and 11 brothers) all bowed down to him.

"That's a fine dream to have!" Jacob scolded him. "You want all of us to bow down to you and kiss your ass?"

And his brothers hated him even more.

One day, Israel said to Joseph, "Go on out to the pastures and check on your brothers and report back to me."

"Yes, Father."

His brothers saw him coming.

"Here comes the dreamer!"

"Let's kill the bastard right now and be done with him!"

"We'll stuff his body down a well and say he was eaten by a wild animal."

"Then we'll see what becomes of his dreams!"

But Reuben protested, "We can't kill him! Sure, stuff him down a well, but don't kill him!" He wanted to save Joseph and return him to Jacob.

His brothers reluctantly agreed.

Joseph is stuffed and stomped down a well

Joseph walked up, maybe smiling or grinning or waving, the Bible doesn't say, but his brothers grabbed him and ripped that fancy tunic off him. Then they dragged Joseph over and stuffed and stomped him down into a dry well!

Then they returned to camp for a nice picnic lunch.

They could probably hear Joseph's muffled screams as they picnicked, but the brothers sat and enjoyed their lunch without that arrogant pain in the ass Joseph ruining it.

Joseph sold to some Midianites and they sell him to Potiphar in Egypt

Presently a caravan of Midianites en route to Egypt appeared in the distance.

Judah said, "Why kill our brother? Why not sell him to these Ishmaelites? He is, after all, our brother."

The brothers agreed and they went and dragged Joseph up from the well and dusted him off. When the Midianites arrived, they sold Joseph to them for 20 shekels of silver. The caravan left with Joseph and he was gone, *poof*, like he had never existed.

What a relief!

Reuben somehow missed all of this, and when he returned and learned of it, he tore up his clothes and cried, "What am I going to do?"

"Calm down!"

"Easy!"

"We'll follow the original plan."

The brothers tell their father that Joseph was eaten by a wild animal

The brothers slaughtered a goat, dipped Joseph's fancy tunic in its blood, brought it home and asked Jacob if he recognized it.
"It's Joseph's tunic!" Jacob cried.
"Father, a wild animal must have eaten him!"
"A wild animal ate my boy!" Jacob wailed. "Tore him to pieces!" And he ripped his own clothes off and mourned in sackcloth, refusing to be comforted, wanting only to die and go down to Sheol (the place of the dead before the invention of heaven and hell) to join his favorite son.

Meanwhile, the Midianites took Joseph to Egypt and sold him to Potiphar, the commander of Pharaoh's guard.

Chapter 38

Yahweh Kills Two of Judah's Boys

About this time, Judah left home, settled in Adullam with a guy named Hirah, married a Canaanite woman, and she gave him three sons: Er, Onan, and Shelah.

Er grew up and married a girl named Tamar, but somehow Er pissed Yahweh off, so Yahweh killed him. This does not appear to have upset Judah much and he simply ordered Onan to pinch hit for Er and fuck Tamar, which, in some convoluted ancient Hebrew logic, continued Er's line.

Onan was happy to fuck Tamar, but did not want her kids, so he always pulled out and squirted his semen onto the ground.

Now THIS pissed off Yahweh, so he killed Onan.

Judah caught on. Two of his sons fucked Tamar and Yahweh killed them both, so Judah got smart; he sent Tamar home to her father so Shelah would not fuck her and get killed by Yahweh.

Time passed, Judah's wife died and when he finished mourning her, he headed up to Timnah to shear sheep with his old buddy, Hirah the Adullamite.

Judah mistakes his daughter-in-law for a prostitute and fucks her by the road

The widow Tamar, still pissed about Judah not assigning Shelah to fuck her as custom demanded, caught wind of this and devised a clever plan. Disguised as a veiled prostitute, she waited for Judah at the entrance to Enaim on the road to Timnah.

Along came Judah and, seeing a veiled prostitute with a nice enough ass, he stopped and inquired, "How much?"

"What will you pay?"

"One goat, but I'll have to send it to you."

"OK, but I'll need a pledge."

"What will you accept?"

"I want your seal, your cord, and your staff."

"Deal!"

You get the feeling it wasn't the first roadside prostitute Judah had fucked. The father of Judaism wound his ass up and fucked his disguised daughter-in-law in the dirt by the road into Enaim like a drunken camel. Unlike his dead son Onan, Judah blew a full load into Tamar and knocked her up good! Finished, he caught his breath, crawled up, tucked little Judah in, and continued on to Timnah, while Tamar went quietly home and resumed her life as a widow, albeit a newly-pregnant one.

True to his word, Judah sent his buddy Hirah with a goat to pay the "prostitute," but Hirah could not find her and no one knew anything about any prostitute working the gates of Enaim, so Hirah finally gave up looking and reported back to Judah.

Judah shrugged and said, "Fuck it. Let her keep the pledge or I'll be laughed at. I tried, but you couldn't find her."

Judah learns that Tamar is a harlot and wants to burn her alive

Three months later, Judah learned the widow Tamar was pregnant and became enraged.

"Bring her to me!" he cried. "I'll burn that slut alive!"

His men ran and found her, but as they were dragging Tamar away, she produced Jacob's pledge and cried, "Ask him, whose seal and cord and staff are these? Tell him, he is the father of my child!"

It seems a little unlikely that she just happened to have Judah's pledge on her, but we'll go with it. And we'll believe that Judah's men let her go and returned home without her and showed Judah the pledge, because the Bible says they did, not that anything it has said so far has turned out to be true, but we'll be good sports.

Judah recognized his stuff, realized that Tamar was right and he was wrong, and lamented, "I'm a fool for not ordering Shelah to fuck Tamar like I should have!"

So Judah let Tamar live.

Meanwhile Tamar was pregnant with Judah's twins. At their birth, a tiny hand appeared and the midwife tied a scarlet thread to it to mark the first-born and then the tiny hand retreated. Then the second-born son popped right out and Tamar named him Perez. Then the first-born son wiggled out with the scarlet thread tied to his hand and she named him Zerah.

Now you might think that the Bible is setting up another first-born Hebrew baby boy to get fucked by his second-born brother, but you will soon realize that this particular lunacy occurs for no apparent reason.

Chapter 39

Joseph as Potiphar's Slave in Egypt

Potiphar, the commander of Pharaoh's guard, saw that Yahweh favored his slave Joseph—and right away I'm skeptical. Potiphar was an Egyptian and Egypt had its own ancient religion, featuring incredible gods and a fantastic afterlife. You think Potiphar or any sober Egyptian gave a rat's ass about some crap Hebrew god called Yahweh? Who killed you for squirting a little semen on the ground? And offered a piss-poor afterlife where you "gathered with your people" in some dark, subterranean shithole called Sheol?

No way is right!

But I'll continue anyway.

Potiphar put Joseph in charge of all his affairs and, as a courtesy to Joseph, Yahweh made Potiphar very rich and gave him Egyptian life by the balls, except for one small thing:

Potiphar's wife begs Joseph to fuck her and he runs off naked

Potiphar's wife got hot for Joseph and begged him to fuck her. Officially, Joseph refused because it was a sin against God, and never mind that it was perfectly fine with God when Judah fucked his daughter-in-law by the road. I'm betting Joseph didn't accommodate Potiphar's wife because she was a pig, but, pig or not, every time she saw Joseph alone it was, "Fuck me! Fuck me! Fuck me!"

It all climaxed (no pun intended) one day when Potiphar's wife grabbed Joseph by his tunic and screamed, "For Osiris' sake! Fuck me!"

Not good old, god-fearing Joseph. He turned and bolted so fast that his tunic ripped off in her hands. Maybe Potiphar had a neighbor and maybe she saw all this and maybe she turned to her husband and said, "Honey, I just saw Potiphar's slave run off down the street naked!"

But who knows?

We do know that this really pissed off Potiphar's wife and she marched right out and found and cornered Potiphar.

"That miserable Hebrew slave of yours burst in on me, ripped off his tunic, and flashed me!" she cried. "I screamed and he ran off down the street naked! Here is that piece of shit's tunic!"

She threw it at Potiphar.

Well, you can imagine his rage! His miserable Hebrew slave flashing his wife! Potiphar had Joseph arrested and thrown into prison, but fear not, Yahweh was on the job. He made the warden like Joseph so much that he put him in charge of the whole goddamn prison. Thereafter, Yahweh made damn sure everything came up roses for the warden.

Yahweh sure has a way with Egyptians, doesn't he? He made Potiphar put Joseph in charge of his house and now he makes the warden put Joseph in charge of the prison. Well, anything is possible in a cartoon, just wait and you'll see.

Chapter 40

Joseph Interprets Dreams in Prison

Pharaoh got pissed at his cup-bearer and his baker and sent both men to prison and Joseph was put in charge of them. One night, both men had confusing dreams and the next morning Joseph noticed they were troubled.

"What's the matter, boys?"

"I had a bizarre dream!"

"Me too!"

"And there's no one here to interpret them!"

"You're in luck, boys!" Joseph said. "Dream interpretation is God's business and I'm in the loop. Tell me your dreams and I'll interpret them for you."

The chief cup-bearer said, "I dreamed a vine had three branches that budded, blossomed, and clusters of ripe grapes appeared. I picked them, squeezed them into Pharaoh's cup for him."

"That's easy," Joseph said. "In three days, Pharaoh will let you out of prison and give your old job back to you. Do me a favor; when you get out, remind Pharaoh to free me, will ya? I don't deserve to be in Egypt or this rat hole!"

Next, the chief baker recalled his dream for Joseph. "I had three trays of pastries for Pharaoh on my head and birds flew down and ate the pastries on the top tray."

"Well," said Joseph. "The good news is that you still have three days to live, but then Pharaoh will hang you and birds will eat the flesh off your bones."

The Bible does not record the chief baker's reaction to this happy news, but three days later it was Pharaoh's birthday and, sure enough, he freed the cup-bearer and hung the baker and I guess birds ate the flesh off his bones.

But the freed chief cup-bearer seemed to forget all about Joseph.

Chapter 41

Joseph Interprets Pharaoh's Dreams

Two years later, Pharaoh dreamed that seven fat cows emerged from the Nile River, followed by seven wretched cows, and the wretched cows ate the fat ones. Then he dreamed that a healthy stalk with seven ripe ears of grain was swallowed by a scorched stalk with seven meager ears. The dreams troubled Pharaoh and he summoned all the magicians and wise men in Egypt, but none could interpret his dreams and ease his mind.

Then the cup-bearer remembered Joseph and told Pharaoh he had interpreted his dream in prison. Pharaoh had Joseph cleaned up and brought to him.

He got right to the point, "I understand that you interpret dreams."

"Not I," Joseph replied. "But God will interpret your dreams."

Again, at that time there was not one Egyptian alive that gave one rat's ass about the Hebrew god. But in the Bible, Pharaoh told Joseph about his dreams and he listened attentively.

When Pharaoh finished, Joseph explained, "God has revealed the future to you. Egypt will enjoy seven years of plenty, followed by seven years of famine. You better tax Egypt one-fifth during the years of plenty and store grain everywhere so your people will not starve in the coming famine and maybe, you know, find yourself a good governor."

Pharaoh and his ministers agreed with Joseph and Pharaoh asked them, "Is there an Egyptian anywhere as godly as this Hebrew, who can govern Egypt?"

None could think of one.

Pharaoh makes Joseph the Governor of Egypt

Pharaoh turned to Joseph.
"Well then, congratulations! You're the new governor of Egypt! No one will shit without your permission! My people will obey your orders and you report directly to me."

Pharaoh put a fine ring on Joseph's finger, dressed him in fine linen, hung a gold chain around his neck, named him Joseph Zaphenath-Paneah, and gave him Asenath, daughter of Potiphera, priest of On, for his wife and he even gave Joseph a fine chariot just like his own.

Joseph, now thirty years old, toured Egypt in the chariot and they shouted "Abrek!" ahead of him as he traveled, meaning, I guess, "Clear the goddamned way! Big shot coming!" And Joseph collected grain and stored it all over Egypt.

Meanwhile, Joseph's Egyptian wife gave him two sons. He named his first-born Manasseh "because God made me forget my brothers fucked me" and his second-born Ephraim "because God made me rich in the country that mistreated me."

Then, as Joseph predicted, the seven years of plenty ended, famine engulfed the world, and Egypt was the only place with food. Joseph rationed it, and people came from all over the world to buy it from him.

From all over the world?

I'm thinking not too many Chinese or Australian aborigines showed up in Egypt four thousand years ago looking for grain. Do you think maybe the biblical writers said this because they did not know anything or anyone existed much beyond the Mediterranean Sea?

Good thinking.

Chapter 42

Joseph's Brothers Arrive in Egypt without Benjamin

Meanwhile, back in famine-ravaged Canaan, Jacob watched his sons sit around and stare helplessly at each other and cried, "Wake up you idiots! There's food in Egypt! Get your asses over there and get us some before we die!"

Jacob kept Benjamin home to protect him and sent his remaining ten sons to Egypt for takeout. Arriving, they found their way to Joseph, but did not recognize their brother. I think I would recognize a brother I grew up with, even if he was dressed like an Egyptian, but no matter.

Joseph, on the other hand, recognized his brothers immediately, but did not let on. Instead, he grilled them through an interpreter, just like he was a real Egyptian.

"Where you boys from?"

"Canaan."

"I think you're spies."

"No way, we're brothers!"

"We came to get food."

"Our youngest brother stayed behind with our father."

"No, I think you're spies, so I will test you: If you have a younger brother at home, you are not spies. One of you go home and fetch him and the rest of you are under arrest until you bring him back to me."

That's some fucking spy test, but the best part is that no one went home for Benjamin. Joseph put his brothers in jail for three days and then said that if they left him one hostage, they could go home with food, but they had to bring their younger brother back to him or be killed.

Now the brothers remembered how they had fucked Joseph.

"I tried to tell you," Reuben said. "Now we have to pay for it."

Understanding every word, Joseph turned away and wept. After he collected himself, Joseph ordered Simeon bound and held hostage. Then he had his other brothers' donkeys loaded with grain and he ordered their payments to be secretly returned in their grain bags, and never mind that Joseph was stealing grain from Pharaoh and giving it to his brothers.

Joseph sends his brothers home to get Benjamin

The donkeys were loaded up, the money was hidden, and the brothers left for home. But that night, one brother found the money hidden in his grain sack and they all panicked, wondering what God had done to them?

When they returned home with the food, they explained to Jacob they had left Simeon hostage until they returned with Benjamin and how they found their payments returned in their grain sacks and they were scared shitless.

Jacob did not care about the money.

He cried, "You're stealing my children! Both Joseph and Simeon are gone and now you want to take Benjamin too?"

Reuben replied, "I promise to bring Benjamin back. If I don't, you can kill both my sons!"

"I can't send Benjamin," Jacob said. "Joseph is already dead and if Benjamin dies I will go down to Sheol with grief!"

Chapter 43

The Brothers Return to Egypt with Benjamin

Jacob worried about Benjamin, but no one worried much about poor Simeon, who apparently remained bound and gagged in an Egyptian prison while his family enjoyed the free food they got from Joseph for what? Days? Weeks? Months? Simeon's plight apparently forgotten? Well, who knows, but it seems they might have moved a little faster to go back and get the poor guy.

Finally, when they finished eating all of the Egyptian takeout, Israel rounded up his sons again.

"Boys," he said. "Better go back to Egypt and get us some more food."

"We have to bring Benjamin with us," Reuben reminded him. "Sorry, but that's the deal."

"Why did you ever tell them about Benjamin?" Israel moaned.

"He kept badgering us about our family, 'How is your father? Have you another brother?' How could we know he would ask to see him? If you want us to live, send the boy with us and we'll be off," Judah said. "I'll take care of him. We could have been there and back twice without all this Benjamin nonsense."

Israel relented, "Take Benjamin with you and may El Shaddai let you bring him and, and ... what's his name?"

"Simeon."

"Simeon, right. May El Shaddai let you bring Benjamin and Simeon back to me safely. Take twice the money you need and return the money you found in your sacks, because it might have been a mistake. As for me, if I'm fucked, so be it."

The boys loaded up gifts for the Egyptians, including food they could have eaten, which doesn't make any sense in a famine, but that's what it says they did, and they went back to Egypt and found Joseph. As soon as he saw Benjamin, Joseph had his chamberlain invite his brothers into his house for lunch.

The boys feared Joseph and they told his chamberlain about the money they found in their grain sacks and that they were returning it.

The chamberlain replied, "Relax boys. We know your money was returned. Your father's god put your money back in your sacks for you."

So God helped Joseph rob Pharaoh?

Interesting...

But, again, I don't think the average Egyptian chamberlain knew anything about the Israelite god and this story stinks of being completely fabricated (and it does turn out to have been plagiarized from an old Egyptian tale), but I will continue, just like it actually happened.

The chamberlain gave the boys water to wash their feet and he fed their donkeys. Then Joseph appeared and his brothers still did not recognize him—their own brother!

Joseph asked them, "How is your father? Is he still alive?"

They bowed respectfully and replied, "He is alive and well."

Joseph regarded Benjamin. "And this must be your youngest brother, the one you told me about. God be good to you, my son."

And nobody thought it odd for the governor of Egypt to invoke the Israelite god?

Then, overwhelmed by the sight of Benjamin, Joseph turned and ran back to his room and wept. After he collected himself, he returned and lunch was served. The

Egyptians would not eat with Hebrews and had their own table, but Joseph sent food from his own plate to his brothers and Benjamin got five times more food than the others.

Everyone feasted and drank freely and we'll assume that Simeon was untied and released for the party, but the Bible doesn't say.

Chapter 44

Joseph Pranks his Brothers

After lunch, Joseph ordered his chamberlain, "Fill their sacks with as much food as they can carry, return each man's money in the mouth of his sack, and put my silver omen-reading cup in the mouth of the youngest son's sack."

This was done and the following morning the brothers departed at daybreak with their donkeys fully loaded.

After a while, Joseph told his chamberlain, "Now take some men and go catch them and ask them why they stole my silver cup and, you know, act like it's a big deal."

The chamberlain and his posse set off after the brothers. When they caught up to them and asked about the stolen cup, the brothers were dumbfounded.

"What do mean?"

"We came all the way from Canaan to return the money we found!"

"Why would we steal his cup?"

"If you find anyone of us has it, kill him and the rest of us will be your slaves!"

The chamberlain began rummaging through their grain sacks, one after another, and he finally pulled the silver cup out of Benjamin's sack, brandished it, and cried, "Just as I suspected! My master's silver cup!"

The brothers were stunned and tore up their clothes in anguished bewilderment! The chamberlain led the thieves back to Egypt and they all fell prostrate before Joseph in their tattered clothes.

"How dare you!" Joseph barked. "I use that silver cup to read omens and to occasionally check the weather! And you bastards stole it!"

"What can we say, my lord?" Judah replied. "God proved our guilt! We're all your slaves, Massa! When do we start picking the cotton?"

"There is no cotton, you idiot! This is the Bible ... not *Gone with the Wind*!"

"Oh yeah; I forgot. Got a little carried away there, my lord. Well ... do you want us to wipe your ass or build you a pyramid or what?"

"I'm not going to enslave all of you," Joseph said carefully, "just the young punk who stole my silver omen-reading cup. The rest of you are free to go. Grab some souvenirs from the Sphinx Gift Shoppe on your way out!"

The brothers hemmed and hawed and then Judah timidly approached Joseph. "Listen, can I have a private word with you? And don't be angry, you're goddamn Pharaoh to us! I just need to speak to you privately, is all."

I guess they stepped aside, the Bible doesn't say, but they must have.

Judah cleared his throat. "Our youngest brother, Benjamin, who stole your silver cup, he's one of two sons from Dad's favorite wife, and the other one was eaten by a wild animal, so Dad didn't want us to bring him; but you said, no young brother, no food, so we had to bring him. I promised that I would protect him, so I'm in a tough spot here. I can't leave the kid here and ruin the old man's life, know what I mean? Is there any way we can work around this?"

Judah wasn't asking, he was begging, and the Bible must have been looking for a cliffhanger, because this chapter ends here.

Chapter 45

His Brothers Discover that Joseph is the Governor of Egypt

Joseph couldn't stand it any longer; he sent the Egyptians away and collected his brothers.

"Boys! Don't you recognize me?" he cried. "It's me, your brother Joseph! I'm here in Egypt and I'm running the whole goddamned country!"

His brothers were astounded.

By god, it WAS Joseph! Last seen being dragged up from a well and sold to the Midianites! I guess that this guy looked and sounded exactly like the guy they grew up with had never tipped them off.

"Don't worry about a thing!" Joseph said. "All that stuffing-me-down-a-well and selling-me-into-slavery and having-me-imprisoned stuff was all God's plan. Now I'm running goddamn Egypt and we're in Fat City, boys! The Egyptians stand in line to kiss my ass! We can do anything we want! It was all God's plan to save us—don't you see? We've had two years of famine and there's five more years to come. I'm here to make sure we all survive!"

Well, it was some fucking plan, that's for sure. Couldn't God have simply ended the famine? Wouldn't that have been a whole hell of a lot easier?

I know.

Anyhow, Joseph told his suddenly jubilant brothers to rush right home and give dad the great news—that he was not only alive, but alive with the keys to goddamned Egypt! By the way, why would Joseph wait for a famine to tell dear old dad that he was alive? And not just running some lousy Bedouin Bed and Breakfast in some godforsaken oasis, but alive and running goddamned Egypt! The greatest nation in the world! I might have wanted my father, and maybe even my mother to know that, wouldn't you?

Meanwhile Pharaoh was so happy to hear about Joseph's happy family reunion that he ordered wagons loaded with food and prizes for Joseph's brothers to take back home with them.

"And tell them, 'Why starve in that shithole Canaan? Come to Egypt! We got plenty of food here and a sphinx and pyramids and a fabulous afterlife! Fuck Canaan! Come to Egypt and I'll give you the best land and all the money and prizes you want!'"

The brothers raced home with their food and prizes and the great news. When Jacob heard it, he did what passed for handsprings when you're 130 years old and declared, "Pack up, boys! We're moving on up to Egypt! I gotta see Joseph before I die!"

And you still hope that someone remembered to untie Simeon and free him.

Chapter 46

Israel Moves to Egypt

Israel packed up the wagons that Pharaoh sent him and moved to Egypt.

On the way, he stopped at Beersheba and sacrificed to Isaac's god, who told him in a vision, "Jacob or Israel—whatever the hell your name is—I am your father's god El. Do not fear Egypt. I will make you into a great nation there and don't worry, I'll bring you back home one day and Joseph will watch you die."

Don't fear Egypt? Are you kidding me? Joseph is running the place and Pharaoh sent wagons to bring him; he's arriving as a goddamned celebrity! And notice, sometimes dad's god is Yahweh, sometimes El Shaddai, and now just El? The head god of Canaan.

When they reached Egypt, Israel sent Judah to Joseph in Goshen to arrange a joyous reunion with the sixty-six family members he brought to Egypt with him so, counting Joseph and his two sons, there were now seventy Israelites in Egypt and the Bible names every goddamned one of them here, but I'll spare you that monotonous roll call.

After the happy reunion, Israel said to Joseph, "Now that I have seen you alive, I can die."

Then Joseph told his family, "I will go and give Pharaoh the good news that you have arrived with all your livestock, but there is one problem: The Egyptians are horrified by shepherds. So when Pharaoh asks, tell him you're shepherds, but remind him that you will stay in Goshen, so it will not be a problem. And don't worry, I'll make it good with him."

Chapter 47

Joseph Introduces His Family to Pharaoh and They Live Happily in Egypt

Joseph went to Pharaoh with the happy news that his family was now in Egypt and he introduced five of his brothers to him.

Pharaoh asked them, "What kind of work do you do?"

"We're shepherds, here to escape the famine in Canaan, and we hope to settle in Goshen."

Pharaoh either told them to settle in Goshen or anywhere in Egypt they wanted, as two versions of the story collide here, and then Joseph brought his father in to meet the great man.

Pharaoh asked Jacob, "How old are you?"

"I'm 130 years old and I have not lived as long or as happily as my ancestors."

That was it.

Joseph and Jacob then left the room and I agree that it was not much of an interview. Joseph settled his father and brothers in Rameses, the best part of Goshen, and Pharaoh had Joseph stuff them with food during the terrible famine.

Meanwhile, Joseph turned the famine into a windfall for Pharaoh by selling food to both the Egyptians and the Canaanites. The people happily begged Joseph to take all their money, livestock, and land in exchange for food until Pharaoh had all their money and owned everything in Egypt, except for what belonged to the priests.

Then the newly impoverished Egyptians begged Joseph to make them serfs. He gave them seed to plant and took 20 percent of the harvest for Pharaoh and the

Egyptians were so happy that it became law that 20 percent of any harvest was Pharaoh's, a law that remains today.

And don't ask me why there is a famine if they can grow food; I'm just repeating the Bible, which says the Israelites acquired land and grew prosperous and numerous in Goshen. I guess either Pharaoh or the priests sold it to them, and does this mean that now all of Egypt was owned by Pharaoh, the priests, and the Israelites? This seems pretty unlikely to me, but the Bible does not say.

Jacob lived seventeen more years in Egypt and one day Israel called Joseph to his bed and said, "If you really love me, place your hand under my thigh and swear that you will not bury me in Egypt, but will take me home and bury me with my ancestors."

Joseph slipped his hand under Jacob's thigh, swore it, and could not cross his fingers under the thigh, so maybe it's not such an idiotic practice after all.

Then Israel sank back onto his pillow.

Chapter 48

Jacob/Israel Blesses Joseph's Sons

Joseph brought his sons Manasseh and Ephraim to visit his dying father.

When Jacob learned that Joseph was present, Israel struggled to sit up in bed and said to him, "El Shaddai appeared to me at Luz and gave me Canaan, so about your inheritance: The two sons born to you before I came to Egypt are mine, just like Reuben and Simeon, but the children born to you since I came to Egypt are yours and will be known by their brothers' names in my will."

I have no idea what this means. Joseph only had two sons, both born before Israel came to Egypt, and I made no attempt to figure this out.

Jacob continued, "Your mother Rachel died in Canaan, on the road to Ephrath, which became Bethlehem, and I buried her by the road..."

Israel, his vision poor, suddenly realized that Joseph had two boys with him. "Who are these guys?" he asked.

"They are my sons born in Egypt, Father."

"Well, I'll be goddamned! Bring them here so I can bless them!"

Joseph put the boys on Israel's lap and he embraced them.

"I thought I would never see you again and here I see your children! Goddamn!"

This does not say much for his grand parenting skills. He's been in town for seventeen years and just met his grandchildren?

Joseph took the boys from Israel's lap and I have to do the math: Both Manasseh and Ephraim were born before

Jacob came to Egypt, so they have to be at least 18–19 years old, and they've been sitting on a 147-year-old man's lap?

Just an observation.

Joseph bowed low and presented the boys for their blessings; Ephraim in his left hand to get Israel's right-hand, first-born blessing and Manasseh in his right hand to get Israel's left-hand, second-born blessing. But to maintain the biblical tradition of fucking the first-born, Israel crossed his hands and placed them on the boys' heads.

"No, Father!" Joseph protested. "Manasseh is the first-born; place your right hand on his head!"

Israel refused.

"I know what I'm doing," he barked, adding, "But don't worry about Manasseh, he will become a great people, but Ephraim will be greater; he will become a great nation."

Then Israel gave this blessing.

"May Abraham and Isaac's god, my guide and protector, bless these boys and fill the earth with my progeny!"

And I ask, is there anything more worthless and useless than a blessing? Sure, maybe a prayer, but I hear a lot of "God bless him or her or this or that" every day, repeatedly, over and over, especially after any kind of a catastrophe and it's all nonsense. You can fly to Rome and get blessed by that quaint visitor from the 15th century, the Pope, then walk out and cross St. Peter's Square, step into the street and get run over by a bus!

That's what good a blessing is!

Anyhow...

After he blessed the kids, Israel said, "I will die soon, but God will take you back to Canaan and he'll protect

you and I will give you a Shechem more than your brothers, the one I took by force from the Amorites."
Whatever in hell that means.

Chapter 49

Jacob's Opinion of His Sons–The Future Patriarchs of Israel

Jacob gathered his sons around his deathbed.

"Boys, before I die, here's what I think of you:

"Reuben, my first-born, you are a wild man who will amount to nothing because you fucked your brother Dan's mother.

"Simeon and Levi, you are murderers who kill men and hamstring oxen for fun; I want nothing to do with either one of you malicious bastards! I curse your rage and I will scatter you throughout Israel!

"Judah, you are a lion; you will dominate your enemies and your brothers will kiss your ass. You'll rule, people will bring you tribute, and you'll wash your clothes in wine."

You might think Judah would interrupt here and ask, "What do you mean, I'll wash my clothes in wine? Are you insane?" But he did not, he let Jacob or Israel, whatever he is being called here, roll.

"Zebulun, you will be a sailor, living by the sea.

"Issachar, you will work like a donkey.

"Dan, you are a snake that bites a horse so its rider falls off.

"Gad, you will get your ass kicked, but you will kick ass back.

"Asher, you will be a good farmer.

"Naphtali, you are a swift hind (female deer) and you will bear lovely fawns..."

Huh?

Though generally senseless, the Bible will occasionally outdo itself and you just have to accept it as incidental, undecipherable stupidity and read on.

Jacob or Israel continued:

"Joseph, you are my favorite son! The Mighty One of Jacob! The Stone of Goddamn Israel! El Shaddai will bless you and you will get two shares of inheritance—one each for your sons, Ephraim and Manasseh.

"Benjamin, you are a voracious wolf who kills in the morning and eats all day."

Such were Jacob's evaluations of his sons, let's summarize them:

Joseph–Great man!
Asher–Good farmer.
Benjamin–Good soldier.
Judah–Born leader.
Zebulun–Ordinary man.
Issachar–Ordinary man.
Naphtali–Meaningless man.
Dan–Snake.
Gad–Bandit.
Reuben–Stepmotherfucker.
Simeon–Violent and despicable man.
Levi–Violent and despicable man.

I note all this in case you assumed the patriarchs of the famous Twelve Tribes of Israel were all great and noble men. Israel himself only had high regard for two of them: Joseph and Judah. He had little regard for five of his sons and he either had no use for or he outright despised his other five sons. His most interesting evaluation was of Levi, whom he despises as a malicious murderer and, yet, it is Levi's lineage who will become the Israelite priests.

Isn't that interesting!

Jacob/Israel dies

"Now," Jacob or Israel declared. "I will die. Bury me with my ancestors in the cave at Machpelah in Canaan that Abraham paid retail for."

Then Jacob or Israel (whichever you prefer) died and was "gathered to his people."

Chapter 50

Jacob/Israel is mourned

Joseph covered his dead father's face with tears and kisses and then ordered him embalmed.

The Egyptians mourned Jacob/Israel for seventy days and then Pharaoh let Joseph take his father back to Canaan for burial, accompanied by his family and all the dignitaries of Egypt, with chariots and horsemen; it was quite a retinue.

Just across the Jordan River, at Goren-ha-Atad, they held a long and solemn lamentation and Joseph mourned seven days there for his father. Watching all this, the local Canaanites called the place Abel-Mizraim.

Then Israel/Jacob's sons carried him to the cave in the field Machpelah and buried him with his ancestors. There was no eulogy—no mention of him stealing Esau's birthright and special blessing or any of his slave-fucking.

When they returned to Egypt, Joseph's brothers worried that with their father dead, Joseph would seek revenge for them stomping him into a well and selling him into slavery, so they sent him this note:

"Before dad died, he said selling you into slavery was no big deal and you should forgive us for doing it."

Joseph wept when he read it.

Then his brothers appeared, threw themselves at his feet, and begged him, "Make us your slaves!"

God turns out to be a lot like Rube Goldberg

"Don't be ridiculous!" Joseph replied. "It was God's plan for you to strip me, stuff me down a well, and then sell me to the Midianites, so they could sell me to Potiphar, so his wife could beg me to fuck her, so he would get pissed and throw me into prison, where I interpreted dreams and Pharaoh found out, and I interpreted his dreams so well that he made me the governor of Egypt. God had the famine all planned and was just protecting us."

It seems to me that all God really had to do was to tell Joseph, "Look, I have a famine planned, so go to Egypt and I'll make you the governor there so you can protect your family."

Simple enough.

And what about this famine business, anyhow? Imagine the pure horror of millions of people starving to death? Browse the Auschwitz yearbook if you need a recollection and then ask yourself: How many mass starvations has God arranged for us? Think about it. First God makes us eat the other life on earth to survive and then, every now and then, just for the hell of it, he starves a few million people.

I mean, you just gotta flat-out wonder about this prick!

Anyhow, Joseph took good care of his family in Egypt. He lived to be 110 years old and saw his grandchildren, though it seems a guy that age would see more generations than three, but that's what the Bible says.

Joseph dies, ending the Egyptian gravy train

Then (I suppose some years later, but who knows, considering how the Bible records time), Joseph called his brothers to him and said, "I'm about to die, but don't worry, God will take care of you. After I die, he will take you back to Canaan, the land he promised to Abraham, Isaac, and Jacob. Make sure you take my bones with you."

It seems a little odd that Joseph, the second-youngest brother, would die before all the others, but again, there is enough serious stupidity to deal with in the Bible, so I won't bother with it. Joseph died at the age of 110 and the Egyptians embalmed him and laid him in a coffin.

No word as to whether or not he was gathered to his people in that shithole Sheol.

To be continued...

Soon to be released:

Holy Bible

The Best God Damned Version

Five Books of Moses

Manufactured by Amazon.ca
Bolton, ON